Gü®

CHOCOLATE
COOKBOOK

Collins

First published in 2012 by Collins
an imprint of HarperCollins*Publishers*
77–85 Fulham Palace Road
London W6 8JB

www.harpercollins.co.uk

10 9 8 7 6 5 4 3 2

A catalogue record for this book is available
from the British Library.

ISBN: 978-0-00-746293-3

Editorial director: Lizzy Gray
Project editor: Helen Wedgewood
Designer: Myfanwy Vernon-Hunt
Food stylist: Kim Morphew
Props stylist: Cynthia Inions
Recipe consultant: Annie Nichols
Photography assistant: Mike English

Printed and bound in Italy by L.E.G.O. SpA

MIX
Paper from
responsible sources
FSC www.fsc.org **FSC C007454**

FSC™ is a non-profit international organisation established to promote the
responsible management of the world's forests. Products carrying the FSC
label are independently certified to assure consumers that they come from
forests that are managed to meet the social, economic and ecological needs
of present and future generations, and other controlled sources.

Find out more about HarperCollins and the environment at
www.harpercollins.co.uk/green

CONTENTS

Welcome to the chocolatey world of Gü   7

Make the most of our recipes   8

... *for* **CHOCOLATEY BASICS**   18

... *for* **BREAKFAST AND BRUNCH**   40

... *for* **TEATIME OR ANYTIME**   58

... *for* **TREATS**   88

... *for* **FEEDING FRIENDS**   114

... *for* **SPECIAL DAYS AND HOLIDAYS**   158

... *for* **CHOCOLATE EXTREMISTS**   188

Acknowledgements   215

Index   216

About the Gü Chefs   224

WELCOME TO THE CHOCOLATEY WORLD OF GÜ

Since Gü first entered the world in 2003, we've had a healthy obsession with all things chocolate. Our deliciously irresistible chocolate puds have become a firm favourite with dessert lovers worldwide and we're always looking for ways to bring even more chocolatey pleasure to our fellow chocolate lovers.

Having made a bit of a name for ourselves in hitting the perfect chocolate spot every time, we started getting lots of requests for our recipes and tips, so we thought, why keep such a good thing a secret? Why not share the love? Couldn't we help you, our fellow chocolate worshippers, to make your own decadent treats at home when you've got a bit more time than it takes to open a ramekin or unwrap a brownie?

So here it is – the first ever Gü chocolate cookbook, which our brilliant chefs have filled with some of our iconic Gü classics as well as lots of must-try new creations. From mousses to millefeuilles, sauces to savouries, crèpes to cakes, brownies to blinis, pancakes to profiteroles, fondants to fondues, tarts to toppings, churros to cheesecakes, ice creams to eclairs, even white chocolate parsnips and chocolate-crusted chickens. You name it, we've gone there in the name of 'chocolate research' (tough work …) and here in the next 200-ish pages are our favourite recipes all using this brilliantly versatile and delicious, humble hero of the store cupboard – chocolate.

We're so excited to introduce you to the next generation of Gü chocolate decadence and trust you will delight in devouring them as much as we've revelled in creating them in the Gü kitchen.

We'd love to know what you think about our new ideas and hear any inspirations for future desserts, so do drop us a line at ilovegu@gupuds.com or show us your creations on www.facebook.com/GuUK.

Seek delight. Give it a go. Give in to Gü – you know you want to …

The Gü team

MAKE THE MOST OF OUR RECIPES

Chocolate is one of the most irresistible of ingredients (well, we would say that, wouldn't we?), whether it is dark, milk or white chocolate. But when it comes to the quality of chocolate, the best way to judge this at home is by the cocoa solids. The higher the proportion of cocoa solids (made from roasted and ground cocoa beans, sugar and cocoa butter), the more chocolatey the taste.

Before you set about making any of our recipes, read through the ingredients list to make sure you have our suggested chocolate stashed away in your kitchen. We think that for dark chocolate, it's best to use a minimum of 50% cocoa solids, but often 70% is preferable. We always give you a recommended level of cocoa solid, but if, say, we suggest 50% cocoa solids and you can only find a chocolate that contains 70%, it would be best to reduce the quantity by 10–15% or the end result will be too rich. Likewise, add 10–15% if you are using 50% cocoa solids rather than a recommended 70%. For milk chocolate, the minimum cocoa solids should be 34%.

White chocolate is a slightly different ingredient as it is made up of very little or no cocoa solids. However, a good white chocolate will have a maximum of 30% cocoa butter. So check out those labels.

USEFUL ADVICE

With each of our recipes we have given you a step-by-step method to show you the best way to create our dishes. However, working on the basis that we like to leave no stone unturned, here is some background information for the skills and equipment that we have used so that you can stun your friends and family each and every time you produce a Gü pud, snack or nibble from these pages.

SOME GENERAL INFORMATION

To kick off, we recommend you read these points before you get stuck into cooking.

OVEN TEMPERATURE: An oven takes a good 10 minutes to heat up to an average 180°C/Gas mark 4, so make sure you leave enough time for this to happen. There's no point in putting your carefully prepared cake mixture in an oven that isn't hot enough. For recipes like sponge cakes and soufflés, gently close the door on your creation and keep it closed as a sudden blast of air into the oven can affect how well they rise.

MEASURING SPOONS: When a recipe calls for a measure in a teaspoon or tablespoon, bear in mind that 1 teaspoon = 5ml and 1 tablespoon = 15ml (or 3 teaspoons).

INGREDIENTS

The freshest ingredients are always the best and for chocolate to keep at its best, store it in a dark and cool cupboard.

MILK: Always use whole milk. This is what we've used for all our testing purposes. Not only does it have the best flavour, but it also adds the necessary consistency. Semi-skimmed or – shock, horror! – fully skimmed milk, will result in a thinner mix so, for example, pastry won't bind so easily and custard won't be so rich. Cooking might be an art form, but it's a science too and we want you to have only the best results.

BUTTER: When you are baking it is always best to use ingredients that are at room temperature as this helps them to bind together better. For butter, it is even more helpful if it has also been softened slightly. If you are cooking on a hot summer's day, there's every chance that your butter will be nicely softened already, but on a cooler day, you will have to help things along. The best way to do this is to put the butter in a microwave and heat it at a medium setting for 10–15 seconds at a time. Check the butter between each blast because it can very easily start melting rather than simply softening.

For the majority of our recipes, we suggest you use unsalted butter as we particularly like its rich, creamy taste. Of course, if you prefer to use the salted variety, that is your choice.

EGGS: As with all fresh ingredients, you will want to ensure that the eggs you use are as fresh as possible (with the exception of meringues, see page 14) and are at room temperature.

All eggs in the recipes in this book are medium sized, unless stipulated otherwise.

WHIPPING CREAM VERSUS DOUBLE CREAM: Our head chef Fred prefers to use whipping cream over double cream because it is lighter and not as rich. Perhaps unsurprisingly, given its name, it whips well and yet is also good as a pouring cream. We like versatility. For all our recipes, we've specified our preference.

If you find it difficult to source whipping cream, you can make your own by mixing double and single cream two thirds to one third.

LEAF GELATINE: Yes, size does matter. Don't be fooled by packets of leaves as their size and strength varies from manufacturer to manufacturer. For this reason, we've given a weight of gelatine (and approximate number of leaves) for each of our recipes that make use of this setting agent.

Never boil any mixture that contains gelatine because otherwise you risk losing its setting properties.

HOW TO MELT CHOCOLATE

You can either melt chocolate in the microwave (our chef Fred's favoured method) or in a bowl over a pan of simmering water (otherwise known as a bain marie). Whichever method you choose, first pop the chocolate pieces into a heatproof bowl. Make sure that they are broken or chopped into equally sized pieces to ensure an even melting.

Fred is a big fan of melting chocolate in the microwave because you are not creating unnecessary heat in your kitchen and the worst enemy of chocolate is humidity. Put the bowl of chocolate in the microwave and heat it in short blasts of 30–40 seconds on a low power setting to avoid scorching or burning the chocolate. Stir the chocolate between each bout of heat. If the bowl you are using becomes too hot for you to handle after it has been microwaved, it is also too hot for your chocolate, so pour it into a cool bowl.

While you can buy a pair of pans that have been specifically designed to nestle together as a bain marie, you can also easily make your own. Choose a heatproof bowl that just sits over a saucepan, but not too far into the pan. Heat some water in the pan to a gentle simmer, then turn off the heat and place the bowl of chocolate over the top. Stir it occasionally as it melts until the chocolate is smooth.

GÜ TIP Make sure that the bowl and any other equipment you are using are completely dry. If any water comes into contact with chocolate as it is melting, it becomes unworkable as it turns grainy and rough in texture.

GÜ TIP Likewise, if chocolate becomes hot when you are melting it, it can become very thick and lumpy. Try whisking in a knob of butter (although this won't help when tempering – see page 193).

HOW TO MAKE CHOCOLATE CURLS

One of the easiest ways to make chocolate curls at home is to use a chocolate bar that has been left at room temperature. Take a metal pastry cutter and scrape it lengthways along the bottom – the flat side – of the bar. This will give you generous large curls to scatter over your chocolate creations.

GÜ TIP Milk and white chocolates are easier to use for curls because there is more fat in the chocolate.

HOW TO BUTTER AND LINE A CAKE TIN

Before lining a cake tin with baking parchment, butter the tin. Be generous with the butter, ensuring that you push it well into any corners (keep hold of your butter wrappers for this, or use pieces of kitchen paper) and up the sides, especially if you are using a fluted tin. For a round, shallow cake tin, you only need to line the base using the bottom of the tin as a template for cutting out the baking parchment. For a deeper cake tin, you may want to line the side as well. Cut a strip of the parchment slightly longer than the circumference of the tin and a few centimetres higher. Fold over one of the longer edges and snip regularly along it. Put this strip into the cake tin first, with the snipped edge running across the base. Cover with the piece of parchment cut out for the base.

If you are lining a loaf tin, cut out a rectangle that is long and wide enough to fit up the sides of the tin. Stand the tin in the centre of the rectangle and draw around the base with a pencil. Then remove the tin and cut into each pencilled corner just once from each side. When you place the paper in the loaf tin and push it down to the base, you will then have four overlapping sections, one at each corner. With a bit of coaxing, they will lie flat around each corner.

BAKING BLIND

In the basic Chocolate Sweetcrust Pastry recipe (see page 29) we explain how to bake a pastry case blind. This means that the pastry needs to be baked completely before the filling is added to prevent it from become soggy. The pastry case is lined with baking parchment and baking beans, which prevents the pastry from rising up when in the oven. After it has been baked for the recommended length of time, remove the parchment and beans from the case and return the pastry to the oven until the base is cooked through.

GÜ TIP You can buy ceramic baking beans, but they are expensive and usually only sold in small quantities. A good alternative is to use dried beans or pulses instead (keep them just for this as they will be inedible, even after the first time you have used them), or you could fill the paper-lined base with a pile of coins. Not only are the coins good and heavy, but they also heat up quickly and speed up the cooking process.

COOKING A CUSTARD

We have given you several custard recipes in this book and for some of our puds a custard forms the basis of the mixture. A custard is a creamy sweet sauce that has been thickened with egg yolks. For the thickening process to happen, the eggs need to be gently heated and stirred continuously. 'Gentle' is the key word here because if you cook the eggs in the sauce too quickly they become thick at the bottom of the pan. Instead of getting a custard, you could end up with a lumpy scrambled mess.

If you think your custard is about to curdle, promptly pour it through a sieve into a bowl and place it in a larger bowl filled with ice to cool it down quickly. Hopefully, this will save the day.

GÜ TIP When you are making custard, warmed milk and cream are poured over whisked egg yolks and sugar and then the mixture is returned to the pan. To avoid burning any residue of the creamy milk when returning it to the pan, leave some of the heated milk or cream in the pan in the first place.

COOKING A SABAYON SAUCE

A sabayon sauce is a light and frothy custard that is cooked in a bowl over a pan of simmering water. As with cooking a custard (see above), the eggs need to be heated in the bowl to thicken the sauce, but gently does it. In contrast to a custard, the eggs are whisked in the mixture rather than stirred so that as much air as possible is incorporated, which helps the eggs to do their thickening job.

GÜ TIP The whisking can easily take 10 minutes, so be patient. The texture you are looking for is a thin trail of the mixture remaining on the surface when the beaters are lifted from the sauce. This is known as the ribbon stage.

COOKING A CARAMEL

A caramel is made by heating sugar in a pan to a rich golden brown colour. The colour is important because otherwise the sugar will be very sweet. Just watch out that you don't cook it for too long as it becomes extremely bitter.

GÜ TIP If you are adding a liquid to the caramel it can splutter and splash, so always cover your arms and hands to avoid being burnt by this extremely hot mixture, stand back and make sure the pan is off the heat.

GÜ TIP To prevent sugar sticking to the side of the pan and burning, use a pastry brush dipped in water to brush down the inside of the pan once the sugar has dissolved and before you bring the syrup to the boil. Alternatively, cover the pan with a lid until it starts to boil, then remove the lid.

MAKING A SUGAR SYRUP

Some of our recipes require sugar syrup that is then heated to 'soft-ball' stage. Heat the sugar and water gently so the sugar can dissolve without burning. It is ready to be further heated once there are no crystals left on the bottom of the pan. Increase the heat and bring the syrup to the boil and then continue to cook to the required temperature.

This is where a sugar thermometer comes into its own (see page 17). As the syrup boils, the liquid evaporates and the sugar levels become more concentrated and so can reach higher temperatures. Soft-ball stage is achieved between 117 and 120°C. Put the thermometer in the syrup before it boils and ensure the base of the thermometer or the probe (depending on what type of thermometer you are using) is covered.

GÜ TIP To accurately read the temperature on a thermometer, make sure that you look at it at the same level as the liquid you are measuring, rather than looking down or up at the thermometer.

MAKING MERINGUES

The most important thing when making meringues is to ensure that the bowl and beaters are spotlessly clean without a hint of grease. If possible, use a glass or stainless-steel bowl as plastic can be more difficult to clean thoroughly. Egg whites can be tricky to work with, so check out the Gü tips, (see below).

When it comes to whisking, beat the egg whites to soft peaks (when you lift the beaters from the egg white, they leave peaks of egg white behind that curl over slightly at the top and although they hold their shape, they will wobble a bit when shaken) before adding the sugar. You are looking to whisk in as much air as possible, so rotate the whisk around the bowl to help volumise the egg white. It also helps to start whisking on a slow setting to introduce small stable bubbles. You can then increase the speed to achieve the required consistency.

GÜ TIP Use older egg whites as they are easier to whisk than fresh ones and when you separate the white from the yolk you must make sure that there isn't any trace of the yolk left.

ELECTRICAL EQUIPMENT

You could fill your kitchen with electrical gadgets and other pieces of equipment designed to make cooking as straightforward as possible, but sometimes we think these can only get in the way. So in our recipes we have limited ourselves to a few pieces of the electrical paraphernalia and, wherever possible, we've given alternatives for doing things by hand.

ELECTRIC HAND MIXER: Also known as an electric hand whisk, these pieces of machinery are inexpensive, store away neatly and are very handy. Some come with different sizes of beater and also a dough hook.

You might want to consider using one with a higher wattage and the number of speed settings that are available.

FOOD PROCESSOR: A good food processor will come with many different accessories, which are helpful for chopping, mixing, puréeing, liquidising, juicing and grinding. Again, the power of the machine will vary, so if you like to use your food processor frequently it might be worth investing in something that is more powerful.

FREE-STANDING MIXER: If you have an electric hand mixer and a food processor, the chances are that you won't need one of these as well, although they do make beating and whisking easier as you have your hands free for other important kitchen tasks.

ICE-CREAM MACHINE: This is certainly a time- and energy-saving piece of electrical equipment. Keep the bowl in the freezer, even when it's not in use, to speed up the whole process. When you are making ice cream, follow the instructions that come with the machine, but remember that as the ice-cream mixture is freezing, it will expand – so don't overfill the bowl.

STICK BLENDER: For the smoothest of sauces, custards and ganaches a stick blender is invaluable. If you don't have one of these, what are you waiting for? Put it on your Christmas list. They are compact, affordable, simple to use and easy to clean.

OTHER USEFUL EQUIPMENT

Most of these pieces of equipment are used regularly in our recipes, so it's worth checking if you need any before getting started.

BAKING PARCHMENT: It used to be the case that you could only buy greaseproof paper for baking, but times have moved on and while greaseproof paper still has its place in the kitchen for wrapping foods like cheese, baking parchment is what you need to use when, well, baking. It is non-stick and comes in a roll to cut to size or you can buy tear-off sheets or circles in various diameters.

Silicone products are also much more readily available, including silicone paper and mats, which can be wiped clean and re-used. The mats are fantastic for lining baking trays and are the perfect base on which to cook our meringues, cookies and choux pastry. You can also buy re-usable silicone cupcake and muffin cases. Just brilliant.

BAKING SHEETS AND TRAYS: This may seem obvious, but a baking sheet has no edges (just possibly a small raised lip along one side), while a baking tray is like a small roasting tin. We give dimensions whenever they are necessary, otherwise use an average sized sheet or tray.

CAKE TESTER: While the traditional way of inserting a skewer into a cake to see if it is cooked through works a treat, you might also like to know of the existence of a heat-sensing tester. The tip turns red when pushed into the centre of a cake and its ready.

MICROPLANE GRATER: In several of our recipes we suggest that you use a Microplane grater as we think they do the best job. These are flat, stainless steel graters that have sharp blades which don't clog – always a boon when grating citrus fruits or chocolate in particular.

PESTLE AND MORTAR: You may associate a pestle and mortar mainly with crushing herbs and spices, but this piece of equipment has other uses, too. In this book you could use it to help make the Citrus Dust and the mint sugar for our White Chocolate Eton Mess (see pages 38 and 148). The heavier the pestle and mortar, the better, and marble and granite are the best choices of material as they are non-porous. They vary in size, too, but for the recipes in this book, you would only need a small pestle and mortar or an electric spice grinder would do the job just as well.

PIPING BAGS: Piping sets are easy to get hold of and come complete with different sizes of straight and patterned nozzles. Silicone or nylon bags are easy to use as they are flexible and quick to clean. Drop your chosen nozzle in place, fill it up and off you go. You can also buy rolls of disposable piping bags that can be cut to fit any size of nozzle or just snip off the end to use on their own. Don't overfill the bags as this will make them difficult to handle, especially if you are doing some fine icing. It is much better to half fill a bag and then come back for more.

RAMEKINS: These little heatproof dishes used to be available in white, white, white or white, but like much else in the kitchen, their design has been revolutionised with the injection of colour and variations in shape: you can even buy heart-shaped ramekins. We are proud of the ramekins that we put some of our puds in, but it is important to note that while we are all for recycling them, they are not designed to be re-heated, so for all recipes in this book that require baking in the oven, please use other shop-bought ramekins of the appropriate capacity.

RUBBER SPATULA: In place of the good old wooden spoon we prefer to use a rubber spatula. They are flexible, come in various shapes and sizes, are easy to clean and kind to non-stick pots and pans. Furthermore, they are also available in wonderfully bright colours so you can choose one to team with your kitchen decor. Not something to overlook. Check what temperature they can be used to. It's best to buy a heatproof spatula for higher temperatures to avoid leaving behind melted rubber in your pans.

SILICONE AND POLYCARBONATE MOULDS: Easy to use, especially when it comes to unmoulding baked goods, these types of moulds are just the biz! If you want to make traditional cakes with specific shapes, such as the financiers and madeleines in this book (see pages 66 and 99), you can buy these soft and durable moulds online or at good bakeware stores. Polycarbonate moulds tend to be used by professional chefs, whereas silicone is more readily available to the home cook.

SUGAR THERMOMETER: One of the most useful pieces of equipment in the kitchen. If you are going to be doing lots of cooking with sugar to make caramel or sweet treats, then it is worth buying a thermometer to help you on your way. Make sure that it has a metal body and that the mercury bulb is low enough for small quantities, but doesn't actually touch the base of the pan so that it reads as accurately as possible. You can also buy digital thermometers that come with a probe to place in the food and an LCD window for reading the temperature (although these won't work on induction hobs).

WEIGHING SCALES: In these days of digital technology, the kitchen weighing scales have not lagged behind. If possible, choose digital scales over the more traditional variety as they are more accurate. They are also easy to clean and don't take up much space. Scales that you can also re-set to zero once you've weighed one ingredient and would like to add another to the same bowl are very helpful, too.

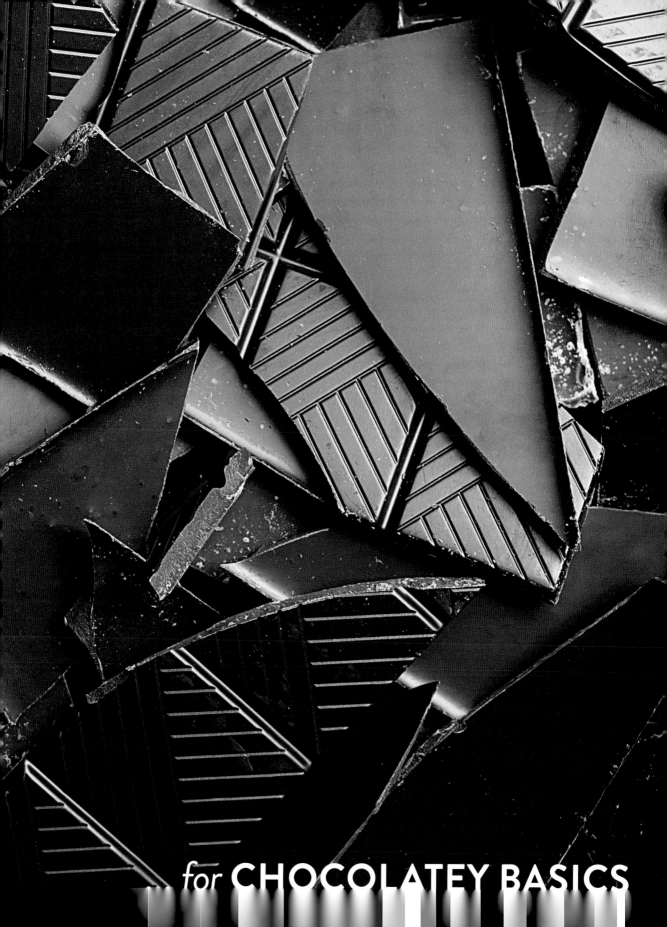

for **CHOCOLATEY BASICS**

CHANTILLY CREAM

Chantilly cream is a sweetened whipped cream that we like to use at any opportunity. Here is the basic recipe (and it really couldn't be simpler) and then throughout the book there are several variations to keep things interesting, see variations below.

MAKES ABOUT 100ML

100ml whipping cream or 60ml double cream and 30ml single cream

2 tsp caster sugar

EQUIPMENT
Electric hand mixer (optional)

1. Pour the cream into a large bowl and add the sugar. Whisk by hand or using an electric hand mixer until it forms soft peaks. Cover with cling film and leave in the fridge until you are ready to use it.

GÜ TIP This basic recipe for Chantilly cream can be further flavoured by adding the seeds scraped from ¼ – ½ of a vanilla pod or the finely grated zest of an unwaxed orange or lime with the sugar. Alternatively, for something a little spicy, add a pinch of ground spices of your choice, like cinnamon or cardamom.

GÜ TIP Throughout this book we have given you several other variations. See:

— Hot Chocolate with Orange Chantilly cream (page 48)
— White Chocolate Eton Mess, which includes a white chocolate Chantilly cream (page 148)
— Profiteroles with Almond Chantilly Cream (page 180)
— Chocolate Millefeuille with Chocolate Chantilly Cream (page 197)

CHOUX PASTRY

WITH A CRISPY CRAQUELIN TOPPING

Here is our definitive recipe for choux pastry topped with a clever secret method to ensure you have crispy choux pastry every time you make it. It's called craquelin and is a very simple pastry that is rolled out thinly and laid on top of the choux pastry before it's baked. You don't have to make the craquelin, but it does ensure a particularly golden and crispy end result.

MAKES 30 PROFITEROLES OR 12–15 ÉCLAIRS

FOR THE CRAQUELIN (OPTIONAL)

50g unsalted butter, softened

60g demerara sugar

60g plain flour

FOR THE PROFITEROLES OR ÉCLAIRS

100g plain flour

100ml whole milk

75g unsalted butter

Pinch of salt

½ tsp caster sugar

3 eggs, beaten

1. If you are making the craquelin, mix together the butter and sugar using a spatula until combined. Then gradually mix in the flour. Roll out the paste between two sheets of baking parchment to about 2mm thick, then place in the freezer for about 30 minutes to set while you make the choux pastry.

2. To make the choux pastry, preheat the oven to 240°C/Gas mark 9. Line two baking trays with baking parchment, putting tiny blobs of the mixture under each corner of the paper to stop it slipping around.

3. Sift the flour into a mixing bowl. Pour the milk into a saucepan with 100ml water and the butter, salt and sugar and bring to the boil. Then remove the pan from the heat.

4. Tip the flour into the boiling mix, all in one go, and beat vigorously with a spatula, until you have a thick smooth paste, and the mixture creates a thin skin around the edges of the pan. This helps to cook the flour and dry out the mixture. It will take about 5 minutes of constant beating back over the heat, which is very important to the finished dish. If you don't beat it for long enough, your choux will be too soft.

5. Leave the cooked paste to cool for a couple of minutes or, if you want to speed up the process, tip it into the bowl of a free-standing mixer and beat for a few minutes to let out the steam.

6. Gradually add the beaten eggs, little by little, beating well after each addition, until you have a smooth, silky and glossy texture. If it looks as though the mixture is separating into glossy lumps, just beat harder and they'll come back together again. Keep testing the consistency as you add each egg, the mixture needs to create a soft peak when poked with your finger.

Free-standing mixer (optional)

Piping bag witted with
a 1cm piping nozzle (optional)

7. Spoon some of the mixture into the piping bag fitted with the nozzle (be careful not to overfill as it will be tricky to pipe out) and pipe out 4cm round profiteroles, leaving a little space around to allow them to rise. Top up the bag as necessary. Alternatively, just spoon out the mixture using a teaspoon.

8. If you are using craquelin, remove it from the freezer and cut out discs or rectangles about 5mm smaller all round than the profiteroles or éclairs, and drape on top of each one to cover.

9. Place the choux pastry in the oven and switch it off for 15 minutes. Then re-start the oven, setting it to 160°C/Gas mark 3 and cook the profiteroles or éclairs for a further 10–15 minutes until they are golden and crispy. Allow to cool completely on a wire rack and fill as described in the recipes suggested, below.

GÜ WAYS TO USE THIS RECIPE We've given you several recipes for profiteroles and éclairs in this book. See the following:
— Profiteroles with Almond Chantilly Cream (see page 180)
— Coconut Snowball Profiteroles with Coconut Snow (see page 190)
— Chocolate Eclairs Filled with Creamy Chocolate Custard (see page 62)

GÜ TIP If you've got more choux pastry than you need, pipe the raw choux onto trays, then freeze them and transfer to an airtight container. Alternatively, freeze the cooked choux buns, defrost and pop back into a hot oven briefly to crisp up again.

THREE CHOCOLATE SAUCES

A well-made chocolate sauce or custard can be the pièce de résistance for any pud. Here we've given you recipes for three of our faves, they're simple, secret weapons to glam up any dessert.

CREAMY CHOCOLATE CUSTARD

First up, an enriched and thickened chocolate custard, that is brilliant as a filling for pastries and perfect as a dessert on its own, served chilled in pretty glasses.

MAKES ABOUT 600ML

4 egg yolks

75g caster sugar

200ml whole milk

200ml whipping cream

175g dark chocolate (about 70% cocoa solids), chopped

1. Put the egg yolks and sugar into a heatproof bowl and lightly whisk them together.

2. Pour the milk and cream into a saucepan, bring to the boil, then quickly whisk two thirds of the mixture into the egg and sugar, and mix well.

3. Pour the mixture back into the saucepan and cook over a very low heat for 5–10 minutes, stirring constantly with a spatula, until it starts to thicken and coats the spatula. You will need to stand with this and stir patiently as it needs to thicken slightly, but watch that the base doesn't get too hot, which will cause it to curdle (see cooking a custard, page 13).

4. Put the chocolate into another heatproof bowl. Remove the pan from the heat and pour it over the chocolate and stir with the spatula until the chocolate has melted and become smooth.

5. Pour the custard directly into serving glasses or dishes. Lay cling film or baking parchment on the surface of the custard to prevent a skin from forming. Leave to cool and then chill for at least 4 hours.

GÜ WAYS TO USE THIS RECIPE To serve, crack some Sesame Nougatine (see page 32) or crumble a couple of cookies (see pages 60, 76, 78 or 109) over the top, or, for something extra special, sprinkle over a little Citrus Dust (see page 38).

SALTED CARAMEL SAUCE

Next is this delicious caramel sauce to serve as a topping for ice cream or drizzle over waffles or even over whipped cream, topping a hot chocolate.

MAKES ABOUT 325ML

2 tsp liquid glucose or runny honey

125g caster sugar

200ml whipping cream

Pinch of sea salt

1. Put the glucose or honey in a saucepan with high sides and warm through over a low heat. Stir in the sugar and 2 teaspoons of water, and simmer gently until is has caramelised and turned a golden brown colour.

2. Warm the cream in another saucepan and set aside. Remove the pan of caramel from the heat and, protecting your hands as it may splutter, gradually and very carefully stir one third of the warm cream into the caramel. Mix together and then stir in the remaining cream.

3. Bring the sauce back to the boil then remove the pan from the heat. Stir in the salt, let the sauce cool down, then transfer it to a bowl and place it in the fridge to chill.

GÜ WAYS TO USE THIS RECIPE We have included this recipe in our White Chocolate Parfait with Salted Caramel and also the Chocolate Salted Caramel and Peanut Tart (see pages 142 and 166).

SALTED CARAMEL CUSTARD

Finally, a custard that is also perfect as a filling for éclairs, profiteroles or other pastries. For a touch of class, the French name for this type of custard is *cremeaux*.

MAKES ABOUT 650ML

4 egg yolks

2 tbsp cornflour

325ml milk

2g gelatine (about 1 leaf)

150g caster sugar

¼ tsp sea salt

200g unsalted butter, softened and diced into small cubes

EQUIPMENT

Stick blender (optional)

1. Put the egg yolks and cornflour together with 4 tablespoons of the milk into a large bowl. Then pour the rest of the milk into a saucepan and gently warm it. Soak the gelatine in a bowl of cold water for 5 minutes to soften.

2. Tip the sugar and salt into another saucepan, this time with high sides, and add 1 tablespoon of water. Heat gently for 3–4 minutes without stirring until the sugar has dissolved and turned a golden brown colour. Remove the pan from the heat and, protecting your hands as it may splutter, gradually and very carefully stir one third of the warm milk into the caramel. Mix together and then stir in the remaining milk.

3. Bring the mixture to the boil, then pour it over the egg yolks and sugar, whisking all the time. Return the custard to the pan and bring back to the boil. Boil for about 30 seconds, stirring constantly, until it has thickened and become smooth. Squeeze out the soaked gelatine and beat it into the custard until it has melted.

4. Leave the custard for about 10 minutes, then add the butter, piece by piece, beating well after each addition, until it has melted and the mixture is smooth. If you've got a stick blender, use it here to blitz the mixture and make it extra smooth.

5. Transfer the custard to a bowl and lay cling film or baking parchment on the surface of the custard to prevent a skin from forming. Leave to cool and then chill for at least 4 hours or overnight.

GÜ TIP You can use powdered gelatine rather than leaf gelatine. Put the powder in a bowl, add 1½ tablespoons of cold water, mix well and then let it soak for 10–15 minutes.

GÜ WAYS TO USE THIS RECIPE Use this custard to fill the Chocolate Eclairs on page 62 instead of the creamy chocolate custard. It is also delicious just as a cream and as a dessert in its own right. Served over roasted or caramelised pineapple and sprinkled with the Chocolate Pecan Crumble (see page 31) it would be perfect for a brunch dessert.

CHOCOLATE SWEETCRUST PASTRY

Here's our recipe for a classic light and crisp pastry, but with chocolate added – of course! You will find that the pastry is used in various recipes throughout the book, which is why we've given you a choice of quantities here. The instructions also describe how to 'blind bake' a pastry case. This means to pre-cook a tart pastry base to give it a good start before you add a wet filling, so it will be nice and crisp once baked with its filling inside.

SMALL QUANTITY
MAKES 24 MINI TARTLET CASES

75g plain flour

pinch of salt

50g unsalted butter, softened

1 lightly heaped tsp cocoa powder

25g icing sugar

1 egg yolk

EQUIPMENT

24-cup mini tartlet tin

LARGE QUANTITY
MAKES 1 X 26CM ROUND TART CASE OR 1 X 20CM ROUND TART CASE WITH SOME SPARE TO MAKE MINI TARTLETS

150g plain flour

pinch of salt

100g unsalted butter, softened

1 lightly heaped tbsp cocoa powder

100g icing sugar

1 egg

EQUIPMENT

26cm or 20cm round fluted tart tin, depending on the main recipe requirement

1. Sift half of the flour into a large mixing bowl, then add the salt and butter and blend together well with a spatula until smooth.

2. Sift the cocoa powder, icing sugar and remaining flour over the butter mixture and rub them in with your fingertips until it forms even-sized breadcrumbs.

3. Beat the egg lightly in a jug and mix this into the flour and butter mix with a fork until it just binds together and forms a dough. (Be very careful not to overmix as the pastry will become tough.)

4. Wrap the pastry in cling film and place in the fridge for 2–3 hours before rolling out.

5. Each of our tart recipes calls for a tart case that is baked blind. To do this, preheat the oven to 170°C/Gas mark 3. Butter the tart tin and cut out a circle of baking parchment that is 10cm larger than the diameter of the tin.

6. Dust a work surface with flour and unwrap the chilled pastry. Roll it out thinly and use it to line the tart tin. Lightly prick the base all over with a fork. Tightly crumple the baking parchment in your hand (to make it easier to fit inside the pastry case), then flatten it and use it to line the pastry case. Fill the base with baking beans.

7. Place the tart tin on a baking sheet and put it in the oven for 10–15 minutes until there is no or a very little wet patch left. Remove the baking sheet and tart tin from the oven, and carefully lift out the paper filled with beans. Then return the baking sheet and tart tin to the oven and cook for a further 10 minutes or until the pastry case is nearly cooked and feels dry.

recipe continues ...

GÜ CHOCOLATE GANACHE

Once you learn to make this easy recipe you'll see what a brilliant all-rounder it is. Ganache is a classic thick chocolate mixture and it can be used hot as a chocolate sauce or dip; cold whisked up as a milkshake, poured over a cake as a shiny glaze, made into truffles, used to sandwich together cookies or macaroons, or chilled and beaten as a fluffy icing for cupcakes. Clever ganache!

MAKES ABOUT 450G

160g dark chocolate (about 50% cocoa solids), broken into small pieces

60g milk chocolate (34% minimum cocoa solids), broken into small   pieces

300ml whipping cream

EQUIPMENT

Stick blender (optional)

1. Put the dark and milk chocolate pieces into a heatproof bowl. Pour the cream into a saucepan and bring it to the boil. Pour it over the chocolate and stir with a spatula until the chocolate has melted and become smooth. If you have a stick blender, then use this to blitz the hot ganache, as it makes the mixture smoother and helps it to set.

2. Use the ganache hot as a sauce or glaze, or pour it into a bowl, leave it to cool and then put in the fridge for 4–6 hours until set. Use as needed.

GÜ TIP The higher the cocoa solids in your chocolate, the firmer your ganache will be.

GÜ TIP If you're feeling lazy you can buy pots of Gü Ganache in the supermarket too.

CHOCOLATE PECAN CRUMBLE

Make this unusual cooked chocolate crumble to scatter over finished dishes to give extra texture and flavour.

MAKES ABOUT 225G

60g pecan nuts

50g unsalted butter, softened

25g demerara sugar

25g light soft brown sugar

2 tsp cocoa powder

60g plain flour

1. Preheat the oven to 140°C/Gas mark 1. Put the pecan nuts in a plastic bag and finely crush them with a rolling pin or other heavy object.

2. Put the remaining ingredients in a bowl and rub them together very well with your fingertips until the mixture resembles fine breadcrumbs. Then stir in the crushed pecans.

3. Spread the mixture evenly on a baking tray and bake for 20–25 minutes or until golden brown. Leave to cool then crumble into small pieces. The crumble keeps in an airtight container for up to 3 days, but you can freeze any leftovers.

GÜ TIP In place of the pecans, use other nuts, like walnuts, almonds, brazil nuts or pistachios – or a mixture of a few.

GÜ WAYS TO USE THIS RECIPE We think this pecan crumble is just the business sprinkled over Chocolate and Pecan Muffins, Boozy Cherry Chocolate Clafoutis or the Pot au Chocolat (see pages 43, 127 and 123). It also makes a great base for either of our cheesecakes (see pages 82 and 160).

SESAME NOUGATINE

This nougatine is a thin, crispy sheet of caramel filled with sesame seeds. It's a brilliant little recipe and can be broken into shards to decorate desserts or crumbled finely over dishes to make them extra special. Use any excess as a delicious seedy snack.

MAKES ABOUT 500G

150g caster sugar

125g unsalted butter, diced

3 tbsp liquid glucose or runny honey

175g sesame seeds

EQUIPMENT

Two 38 x 30cm baking sheets

1. Preheat the oven to 180°C/Gas mark 4 and line the baking sheets with baking parchment or reusable silicone baking mats. Cut two more sheets of baking parchment to the same size.

2. Put the sugar, butter, glucose or honey and 2 teaspoons of water in a heavy-based saucepan and place over a medium-low heat. Bring to the boil, then reduce the heat and simmer until the sugar has dissolved and the mixture binds together. Remove the pan from the heat and stir in the sesame seeds.

3. Pour the mixture evenly between the baking sheets. Place a piece of the baking parchment on top of each and use a rolling pin to roll the mixture thinly to 1–2mm thick. Leave to cool slightly and peel off the top sheets of paper.

4. Bake for 5–10 minutes until they are golden brown, turning the trays once to ensure even cooking. Remove from the oven and leave to cool until solid, then break into small shards and store in an airtight container.

GÜ TIP   The mixture can be made ahead (up to the end of Step 3) and frozen raw in sheets to be cooked as needed.

GÜ WAYS TO USE THIS RECIPE   For an after-dinner treat, make our Gü Chocolate Ganache using 70% chocolate instead of the 50% (see page 30) and pour it into a square dish or tin lined with baking parchment. Allow to cool then set in the fridge. Cut the chilled ganache into little squares and decorate each with a shard of this sesame nougatine.

GÜ WAYS TO USE THIS RECIPE   Use the sesame nougatine shards to decorate the Raspberry Ganache Tart (see page 120) or crumble the nougatine over the Chocolate Stuffed Crust Pizza or the Chocolate and Peach Knickerbocker Glories (see pages 208 and 178).

CARAMELISED POPCORN OR PUFFED RICE

Popcorn needn't be reserved just for trips to the cinema, it's great fun to add to a wide variety of goodies. For some ideas, see our suggestions below.

MAKES ABOUT 3 LARGE HANDFULS

2 tbsp caster sugar

15g unsalted butter

3 large handfuls (about 15g) cooked plain popcorn or 25g puffed rice

1. Line a baking tray with baking parchment, then tip the sugar into a saucepan and add 1 teaspoon of water. Heat gently for 3–4 minutes without stirring until the sugar has dissolved and turned a golden brown colour.

2. Stir in the butter until it melts, then remove the pan from the heat and stir in the popcorn or puffed rice to coat evenly. Scrape out onto the lined tray and leave to cool. The popcorn keeps in an airtight container for up to 4 days.

GÜ WAYS TO USE THIS RECIPE Popcorn or puffed rice cooked in this way can only ever add another layer of pleasure to such recipes as the Caramelised Banana Split with Warm Rum Chocolate Ganache and the Chocolate Fondue (see pages 103 and 165).

CANDIED CITRUS FRUIT

You haven't tasted candied fruit until you have tasted this candied fruit. In fact, maybe you've never tried it at all but trust us – you should! It is truly delicious, succulent and juicy. It can also be made with any citrus fruit that you choose. To serve as sweet treats with coffee or as a cool gift, thoroughly drain pieces of the candied fruit then dip in melted dark chocolate and place on a piece of baking parchment in the fridge to set.

MAKES ABOUT 500G

3 unwaxed oranges or 2 pink grapefruit

Pinch of salt

500g caster sugar

1. Wash the fruit, cut the oranges into quarters or the grapefruit into eighths and place in a saucepan. Add the salt and cover with cold water. Bring to the boil, drain and repeat this twice more (without adding more salt).

2. Pour the sugar into the cleaned pan with 1 litre of cold water. Bring to the boil, stirring to dissolve the sugar, then add the blanched oranges, cover with a lid and simmer very gently for 3 hours. After this time the oranges will be translucent and very soft, and the syrup will have thickened slightly.

3. Leave to cool and then place in the fridge overnight to firm up. Keep in an airtight container or a sterilised jar.

GÜ WAYS TO USE THIS RECIPE Recipes in the book that would love to be topped with these tasty morsels are the Chocolate Financiers, Jaffa Cake Lollipops and the Chocolate, Ginger and Sesame Cookies (see pages 66, 74 and 76). Or use them to dip into our Chocolate Fondue (see page 165).

CARAMELISED NUTS

Mmmm! More goodies to add a little something extra to a recipe, we suggest you scatter these nuts over the Chocolate Waffles or the Melting Chocolate Bombe (see pages 46 and 206). Alternatively, use them instead of the caramel in the Floating Islands (see page 50).

MAKES ABOUT 500G

200g caster sugar

300g nuts, such as pecans, blanched almonds, skinned hazelnuts, peanuts, walnuts or pistachios, or a mixture

EQUIPMENT

Sugar thermometer (optional)

1. Line a baking tray with baking parchment. To make the caramel, tip the sugar into a saucepan and add 2 tablespoons of water. Heat gently for 3–4 minutes without stirring until the sugar has dissolved, then increase the temperature to medium and bring to the boil. Continue to heat the syrup until the sugar thermometer reads 117–120°C (this is known as the soft-ball stage; see page 14 for checking that this has been reached, especially if you don't have a sugar thermometer).

2. Tip the nuts into the caramel and keep stirring on a low heat. At first the sugar will crystallise and look white and hard, but keep stirring because it will soon start to melt and become a golden caramel once again and coat the nuts. Be careful not to burn the nuts or they will become bitter.

3. Tip the caramelised nuts out onto the lined tray and leave to cool. The nuts keep in an airtight container for up to 1 week.

GÜ TIP For the sugar thermometer-free amongst you, to test that a syrup or caramel has reached soft-ball stage, lift a tiny drip of the mixture with a fork and drop it into a cup of cold water. Then pick the sugar out of the water with your fingers and if you can squeeze it easily, like soft toffee, then it's ready. If you can't squeeze it and it feels a little like jam, then try again a minute later.

CITRUS DUST

This is a clever yet dead-easy powder made by drying the zest from citrus fruit. Use it to sprinkle over your chocolate desserts. You can use other citrus fruit or to get truly decadent try lime zest with gin, lemon with vodka, or pink grapefruit with Campari.

MAKES ABOUT 2 TBSP

2 large oranges

70ml Grand Marnier

EQUIPMENT

Electric spice grinder (optional)

1. Finely grate the zest from the orange into a small saucepan, being very careful not to include any of the bitter white pith.

2. Pour the Grand Marnier over the zest and bring to a simmer. Remove the pan from the heat, leave it for 5 minutes for the flavour to infuse and then pass the mixture through a fine sieve. Set the sieve with its valuable contents to one side and keep the resulting sticky liquid in the fridge ready to drizzle over desserts, stir into hot chocolate, whip up with cream (see page 48) or use to make a cocktail.

3. Preheat the oven to its lowest setting. Line a baking tray with baking parchment and spread the zest out evenly. Bake for about 30 minutes or until the zest is almost dry.

4. Remove the zest from the oven and leave to cool, then grind it to a fine powder in a pestle and mortar or put the zest in a plastic bag and crush it with a rolling pin. If you have an electric spice grinder this would also do the job well. The citrus dust keeps in an airtight container for up to 4 days.

GÜ EQUIPMENT A Microplane is a fantastically useful piece of equipment when it comes to grating citrus fruit (see page 16).

GÜ WAYS TO USE THIS RECIPE Scattered over the Chocolate Mousse and Chocolate Truffles (see pages 90 and 92–5), added to the top of a hot chocolate (see pages 48–9), or mixed with the sugar to coat the Churros (see page 44) are just a few suggestions for ways to use this versatile decoration.

... *for* **TEATIME OR ANYTIME**

CHEWY DOUBLE CHOCOLATE COOKIES

These cookies have not only a crisp sweet crust but also a sweet, soft and beautifully chewy middle. The trick is to make the dough the day before as the longer you leave it, the chewier the end result. If you use the dough straight away, you will have a crunchier cookie.

MAKES ABOUT 30

150g unsalted butter, softened

225g light soft brown sugar

1 egg, lightly beaten

1 tsp vanilla extract

225g plain flour

4 tbsp cocoa powder

½ tsp bicarbonate of soda

¾ tsp baking powder

Pinch of sea salt

275g dark chocolate (about 70% cocoa solids), finely chopped or use the same weight of chocolate drops

EQUIPMENT

Food processor or an electric hand mixer

1. Cream together the butter and sugar in the bowl of a food processor or with an electric hand mixer for about 5 minutes until they are light and fluffy. Add the egg and vanilla, and mix again until they are well combined.

2. Sift the flour, cocoa powder, bicarbonate of soda, baking powder and salt into a large bowl. Stir in the wet ingredients until just combined, being careful not to overmix. Then mix in the chocolate, cover and put in the fridge for at least 24 hours.

3. If the dough is too hard to handle once it is chilled, leave at room temperature for 20–30 minutes to soften slightly. Preheat the oven to 170°C/Gas mark 3 and line a couple of baking trays with baking parchment.

4. Roll the cookie dough into about 30 evenly-sized pieces, roughly the size of a walnut in its shell, and place them on the prepared trays, allowing them space to expand.

5. Bake for 12–14 minutes until crisp on top but still soft in the middle. Remove from the oven and transfer the cookies, still on the baking parchment, to a wire rack to cool.

GÜ TIP You can freeze the balls of raw dough. Freeze them in a single layer, then place in a container once solid. Thaw for 10–15 minutes, then place the balls on baking trays and bake as above. They may take a minute or two longer to cook.

GÜ TIP In place of the dark chocolate, use chopped milk or white chocolate and also add the zest of a finely grated orange or a handful of chopped nuts to the mix – use whatever you have in your store cupboard.

CHOCOLATE ÉCLAIRS

FILLED WITH CREAMY CHOCOLATE CUSTARD

Fresh choux pastry generously filled with a rich dark chocolate custard and then topped with melted dark chocolate – what's not to love as a perfect teatime treat? They are something that any master baker would be proud of but are really not that tricky.

MAKES 12–15

1 quantity Choux Pastry Éclairs (see page 22)

300g dark chocolate (about 70% cocoa solids), broken into small pieces

FOR THE CREAMY CHOCOLATE CUSTARD

4 egg yolks

50g caster sugar

40g cornflour

400ml whole milk

200ml whipping cream

275g dark chocolate (about 70% cocoa solids), chopped

EQUIPMENT

Stick blender (optional)

Piping bag fitted with a 5mm piping nozzle

1. To make the creamy chocolate custard, beat the egg yolks with the sugar, cornflour and about 4 tablespoons of the milk to create a smooth paste.

2. Pour the remaining milk and cream into a saucepan and bring to the boil. Pour a quarter of this onto the egg mixture, whisking continuously until smooth, then whisk in the rest. Pour the custard into a clean pan and simmer for 2–3 minutes, stirring continuously, until it has thickened.

3. Remove the pan from the heat, add the chopped chocolate and stir with a spatula until the chocolate has melted and become smooth. Blitzing the custard with a stick blender at this stage makes it even smoother and shinier.

4. Scrape the mixture into a bowl, cover the surface with cling film or baking parchment, to stop a skin forming, leave to cool, then chill in the fridge for 3 hours or preferably overnight.

5. Make the choux pastry éclairs as described on page 22 and leave to cool on a wire rack.

6. At the base of each éclair, make two small holes using the tip of a knife. Fill the piping bag fitted with a nozzle with the chocolate custard (be careful not to overfill as it will be tricky to pipe out), then pipe the mixture into the holes until each éclair is fully filled. Top up the bag as necessary.

7. Melt the chocolate (see page 10). Carefully pour a spoonful of the melted chocolate over each éclair and sit them back on the wire rack for the chocolate to set. Alternatively, dip the tops of the éclairs into the sauce and then place chocolate-side up on a wire rack. If you need to speed up the setting time, pop the éclairs in the fridge.

GÜ TIP   Instead of using the chocolate custard to fill the éclairs, be a bit more adventurous and try the Salted Caramel Custard (see page 27).

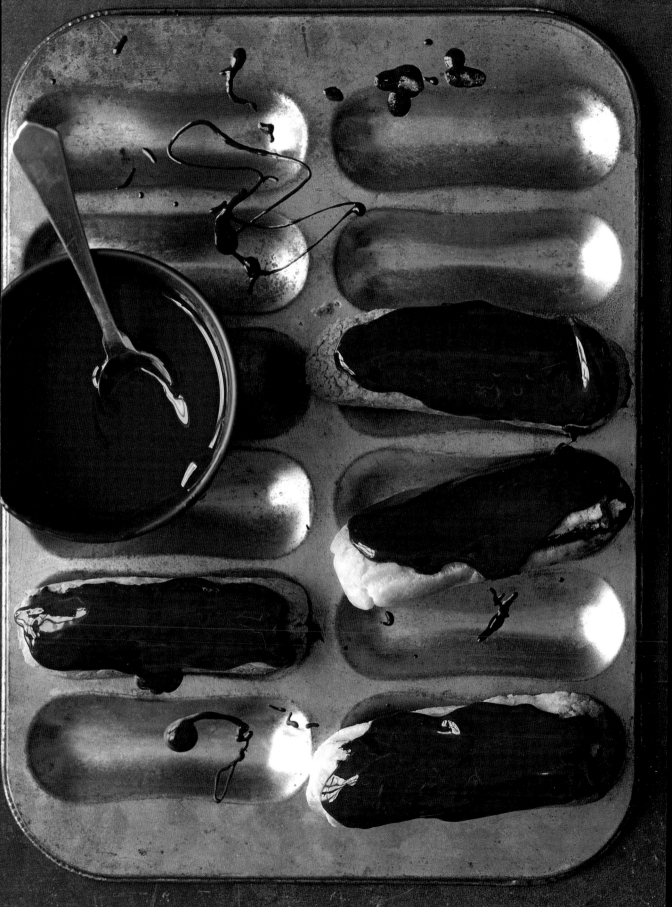

GÜPCAKES

WITH CHOCOLATE GANACHE FROSTING

Our güpcakes are cheeky little numbers: a light and fluffy chocolate sponge topped with a chocolate frosting. They can easily be glammed – add a sprinkle of chopped toasted hazelnuts over the icing, or scatter some Chocolate Pecan Crumble or add shards of Sesame Nougatine (see pages 31 and 32).

MAKES ABOUT 8 FULL-SIZE CUPCAKES OR 15 MINI VERSIONS

FOR THE CHOCOLATE GANACHE ICING

100g dark chocolate (about 50% cocoa solids), broken into small pieces

50g milk chocolate (34% minimum cocoa solids), broken into small pieces

150ml whipping cream

100g unsalted butter, softened

150g icing sugar

FOR THE GÜPCAKES

75g plain flour

1 tbsp cocoa powder

½ tsp baking powder

75g caster sugar

50g unsalted butter, softened

1 egg, lightly beaten

50ml whole milk

EQUIPMENT

12-cup muffin tin or 24-cup mini muffin tin

Cupcake papers or baking parchment

Food processor or electric hand mixer

1. Line your cupcake tins with papers. If you don't have cupcake papers, brush eight cupcake tins with a little butter and cut eight 12cm squares of baking parchment (or 8cm squares for mini cupcakes) and press into the cupcake tins. The paper will rise up but will drop down once you add the cake mixture.

2. To make the chocolate ganache icing, put the dark and milk chocolate pieces into a heatproof bowl. Pour the cream into a pan and bring it to the boil. Pour it over the chocolate and stir with a spatula until the chocolate has melted and become smooth. Leave to cool completely, then put in the fridge to chill.

3. Cream together the butter and sugar in the bowl of a food processor or with an electric hand mixer for about 5 minutes until they are light and fluffy. Then beat in the cooled chocolate mixture and return to the fridge until ready to use, beating it again if it sets too hard.

4. To make the güpcakes, preheat the oven to 160°C/Gas mark 2–3 and sift the flour, cocoa powder and baking powder together into a bowl.

5. Beat the sugar and butter together in another bowl until light and fluffy. Gradually add the egg, little by little. If it looks like the mixture might curdle, then add a little of the flour mixture, which should bring it together.

6. Lightly fold in the flour and cocoa powder mixture and then stir in the milk. Spoon the mixture evenly between the paper cases and bake for 10–15 minutes for the larger cupcakes, and 8–10 minutes for the mini cupcakes, or until a skewer is inserted in the centre it comes out clean. Leave to cool for 5 minutes, then transfer them onto a wire rack to cool completely before adding the icing (you may want to use a piping bag and a nozzle for more accurate icing).

recipe continues ...

GÜ TIP If the icing mixture should curdle when you whip it, it could be because the mixture is too cold. If this happens, scrape it into a saucepan, place over a low heat (or heat briefly in a microwave) until melted. Then pour it into a bowl, leave to set and chill again. Once chilled, beat again until light and fluffy.

GÜ TIP Top the güpcakes with Milk Chocolate or Almond Chantilly Cream instead of the icing (see pages 197 and 180) or use 3 pots (1 box) of our Chocolate Ganache Mini Puds for the icing. Just beat their contents with the butter and icing sugar until light and fluffy and use immediately.

CHOCOLATE FINANCIERS

These delicate cakes are traditionally made in little rectangular tins so that they resemble gold bars, hence the name. They are just as good made in mini muffin tins, although if you want to be purist about these things, then financier silicone moulds are available. We just thought we'd stick to mini muffin tins for ease. The browned butter that is described in the method gives these cakes a gorgeously sweet and nutty flavour.

MAKES ABOUT 24

200g unsalted butter

5 egg whites

150g granulated sugar

60g ground almonds

60g plain flour

50g dark chocolate (about 70% cocoa solids), finely chopped

Finely grated zest of 1 orange

50g toasted hazelnuts, crushed

EQUIPMENT

24-cup mini muffin tin

1. Melt the butter in a saucepan on a medium heat and then cook it until the butter caramelises and takes a golden brown colour. Strain the butter carefully through a sieve into a bowl, leaving behind any burnt bits.

2. Lightly whisk the egg whites in a bowl until they are foamy (this doesn't take long, so a hand whisk will do the job), stir in the sugar and then the ground almonds. Sift the flour over the top and stir all together well with the chocolate and orange zest. Then finally stir in the brown butter.

3. Leave the mixture to rest for at least an hour in the fridge. Preheat the oven to 180°C/Gas mark 4. Spoon the mixture into the tin, sprinkle with the crushed hazelnuts and bake for 12–15 minutes or until when gently touched with your finger the mixture bounces back.

GÜ TIP Stir chopped Candied Citrus Fruit (see page 36) and pistachios or some dried cherries into the mix. For the more daring among you, finely chop a small chunk of fresh pineapple and stir it into the mixture with a few chopped thyme leaves.

WHITE CHOCOLATE BLONDIES

Blondies are gü-ey little nibbles that are brilliant as a teatime treat, but equally marvellous served as a dessert with some fresh crushed raspberries.

MAKES 16

100g unsalted butter

40g honey

280g white chocolate, broken into small pieces

4 eggs

180g caster sugar

190g plain flour

½ tsp baking powder

EQUIPMENT

20cm square cake tin

1. Preheat the oven to 170°C/Gas mark 3 and butter and line the cake tin with baking parchment.

2. Tip the butter, honey and chocolate into a pan, place over a very low heat and stir occasionally until melted.

3. Lightly beat the eggs with the sugar in one bowl and sift the flour with the baking powder into another.

4. Once the chocolate mixture has melted, stir in the eggs and sugar, then carefully fold in the flour mix.

5. Pour the mixture into the prepared tin and bake for 20–25 minutes or until lightly golden on the surface, but soft and fudgy on the inside.

6. Remove from the oven and leave to cool in the tin for 5 minutes before lifting out onto a wire rack. Cut into 16 squares and share them among your friends and family – with or without some raspberries.

GÜ TIP Blondies have even more fun if you stir some chopped white chocolate into the mix just before baking.

CHOCOLATE MARZIPAN CAKE

What a gorgeously gutsy cake this is – a serious chocolate hero of a cake. The marzipan makes it very rich and the chocolate glaze adds a real sense of luxury. Best to eat this one with a fork – so why not get out your best china to really make an occasion out of it?

SERVES 10–12

100g unsalted butter

180ml milk

175g marzipan

100g dark chocolate (about 70% cocoa solids), broken into small pieces

5 eggs, beaten

150g caster sugar

50g cocoa powder

200g plain flour

1 tsp cinnamon

½ tsp baking powder

50g pistachios, chopped

FOR THE GLAZE

125g dark chocolate (about 50% cocoa solids), broken into small pieces

100ml whipping cream

25g unsalted butter, cut into cubes

EQUIPMENT

900g loaf tin

Electric hand mixer

1. Preheat the oven 170°C/Gas mark 3. Butter and line the loaf tin with baking parchment. Melt the butter in a saucepan and set aside to cool.

2. Warm the milk in a saucepan, crumble in the marzipan and then drop in the pieces of chocolate. Whisk with an electric hand mixer until the marzipan has dissolved and the chocolate has melted.

3. Beat the eggs into the chocolate mixture, a little at a time, then stir in the sugar. Sift the cocoa powder, flour, cinnamon and baking powder into a bowl and mix well into the chocolate mixture. Finally fold in the cooled butter and the chopped pistachios.

4. Spoon the mixture into the prepared tin, level the surface and bake for about 1 hour–1 hour 20 minutes or until when a skewer is inserted in the centre it comes out clean. Leave to cool in the tin for 5 minutes, then turn out onto a wire rack, right-side up and leave to cool completely.

5. For the glaze, put the chocolate pieces into a heatproof bowl. Pour the cream into a saucepan and bring it to the boil. Pour it over the chocolate and stir with a spatula until the chocolate has melted and become smooth. Then beat in the butter, a cube at a time, until it is well incorporated.

6. Place the cake on the wire rack over a baking tray and pour the glaze evenly over the cake while it is still warm. Leave to set.

GÜ TIP Like most dense cakes, this one is better eaten the day after it is made. So as soon as it has cooled down, wrap it in cling film and store in an airtight tin.

GÜ TIP Soak a handful of raisins in a little warm rum for about an hour, and stir into the mix with the pistachios.

MACADAMIA NUT BROWNIES

The brownie is like a little black dress for chocolate lovers – it's a lunch box snack, a mid-afternoon bite, a perfectly wrapped pressie or a decadent warm dessert. You can dress them up or down as the mood takes you. This delicious recipe gives you that ultimate versatile brownie – soft and fudgy in the middle with a lovely crisp crust. Check them regularly after they have been cooking for 10 minutes. The surface should have a thin crust, but the middle should still be soft – that is when they are at their most pleasurable.

MAKES 16

240g dark chocolate (about 50% cocoa solids), broken into small pieces

140g unsalted butter, diced

2 tbsp double cream

4 eggs

210g granulated sugar

100g plain flour

4 tbsp cocoa powder

100g macadamia nuts, roughly chopped

EQUIPMENT

20cm square baking tin

1. Preheat the oven to 170°C/Gas mark 3 and butter and line the baking tin with baking parchment.

2. Put the chocolate pieces into a heatproof bowl and set it over a pan of simmering water. Add the butter and cream, then remove the pan from the heat and leave, stirring occasionally, until its contents has melted.

3. Lightly beat the eggs with the sugar in a large bowl, then stir in the melted chocolate mixture. Sift the flour and cocoa powder together and carefully fold in. Finally fold in the chopped macadamia nuts.

4. Scrape the mixture into the lined tin, level the surface and bake for 12–15 minutes or until the surface is dry but the middle still fudgy. Remove from the oven and leave to cool in the tin for 5 minutes before turning out onto a wire rack to cool completely. Cut into 16 squares and see how long you can make them last – we reckon a day at the most.

GÜ TIP Don't feel that you have to stick to macadamia nuts; pecans or toasted peanuts, which have also been chopped, will be just as tasty. Salted peanuts wouldn't go amiss, either. And if it's nuts that you like, consider sprinkling our Chocolate Pecan Crumble (see page 31) over the top just before baking.

GÜ TIP For nut-free brownies (always useful to know about if someone with a nut allergy arrives on your doorstep), replace the nuts with some finely chopped cubes of white chocolate, dates or prunes, or dried figs or cherries.

JAFFA CAKE LOLLIPOPS

Everyone loves a Jaffa cake and here's our lollipop version to add a fun twist. Try using a variety of different coloured sticks or skewers to jazz up your cakes – these little mouthfuls are great for party food.

MAKES ABOUT 48

½ quantity Chocolate Financier (see page 66, leave out the hazelnuts and make in a 18 x 22cm cake tin), or bought sponge cake

1 quantity Candied Citrus Fruit (see page 36) or ½ jar of marmalade

150g dark chocolate (about 70% cocoa solids), broken into small pieces

2 tbsp rapeseed or sunflower oil

EQUIPMENT

2 x 24-cup mini muffin tin or ice cube trays (rubber or silicone would make this even easier), or you could do this in a couple of batches

48 lollipop sticks or wooden skewers

1. Bake the financier sponge in a 18 x 22cm cake tin, then leave it to cool and cut off the crusts.

2. If using the Candied Citrus Fruit, cut each wedge of candied orange into 7–8 pieces (you need 48 pieces in total) and place a piece, skin-side down, in the base of each muffin tin hole or in the ice cube trays. Cut the sponge into 48 little squares and top each piece of candied orange with a piece of sponge, and press lightly. Insert a lollipop stick or wooden skewer into each cube.

3. If using marmalade, then spread this evenly over the surface of the sponge then cut into 48 squares and place these, marmalade-side up, in each muffin tin hole or in the ice cube trays. Insert a lollipop stick or wooden skewer into each cube.

4. Place the tins or trays in the freezer for at least 2 hours. Line a baking tray with baking parchment.

5. Melt the chocolate (see page 10) and stir in the oil. Dip each frozen lollipop into the warm chocolate, tapping off any excess, and place onto the lined baking tray. Pop into the fridge for 20–30 minutes to set completely before serving. (They will also defrost in this time.)

CHOCOLATE, GINGER & SESAME COOKIES

For these grown-up cookies we've combined fragrant ginger and nutty sesame, which give a wonderful aromatic bite. Just like the Chewy Double Chocolate Cookies, these cookies are chewier if you make the dough the day before, and you can also freeze the dough prior to baking them (see page 60).

MAKES ABOUT 30

150g unsalted butter, softened

225g light soft brown sugar

1 egg, lightly beaten

1 tsp vanilla extract

225g plain flour

4 tbsp cocoa powder

½ tsp bicarbonate of soda

¾ tsp baking powder

Pinch of sea salt

2 knobs stem ginger, finely chopped

25g toasted sesame seeds

SPECIAL EQUIPMENT

Food processor or electric hand mixer

1. Cream together the butter and sugar in the bowl of a food processor or with an electric hand mixer for about 5 minutes until they are light and fluffy. Add the egg and vanilla, and mix again until they are well combined.

2. Sift the flour, cocoa powder, bicarbonate of soda, baking powder and salt into a large bowl and drop in the ginger and sesame seeds. Stir in the wet ingredients until just combined, being careful not to overmix. Cover and put in the fridge for at least 24 hours.

3. If the dough is too hard to handle once it is chilled, leave at room temperature for 20–30 minutes to soften slightly. Preheat the oven to 170°C/Gas mark 3 and line a couple of baking trays with baking parchment.

4. Roll the cookie dough into about 30 evenly sized pieces, roughly the size of a walnut in its shell, and place them on the prepared trays, allowing them space to expand.

5. Bake for 12–14 minutes until brown but still soft in the middle. Remove from the oven and transfer the cookies, still on the baking parchment, to a wire rack to cool.

GÜ TIP In place of the ginger, how about adding some chopped Candied Citrus Fruit (see page 36)?

CHOCOLATE, PEANUT & NOUGAT COOKIES

Pieces of sweet nougat and salty peanuts are an unexpected but fab combination in these cookies. Try other nuts, such as macadamia or pecan, for a varied crunchy experience.

MAKES ABOUT 30

150g unsalted butter, softened

225g light soft brown sugar

1 egg, lightly beaten

1 tsp vanilla extract

225g plain flour

4 tbsp cocoa powder

½ tsp bicarbonate of soda

¾ tsp baking powder

Pinch of sea salt

50g salted roasted peanuts, chopped

75g nougat, finely chopped

EQUIPMENT

Food processor or electric hand mixer

1. Cream together the butter and sugar in the bowl of a food processor or with an electric hand mixer for about 5 minutes until they are light and fluffy. Add the egg and vanilla, and mix again until they are well combined.

2. Sift the flour, cocoa powder, bicarbonate of soda, baking powder and salt together into a large bowl and drop in the chopped peanuts and the nougat. Stir in the wet ingredients until just combined, being careful not to overmix. Cover and put in the fridge for at least 24 hours.

3. If the dough is too hard to handle once it is chilled, leave at room temperature for 20–30 minutes to soften slightly. Preheat the oven to 170°C/Gas mark 3 and line a couple of baking trays with baking parchment.

4. Roll the cookie dough into about 30 evenly sized pieces, roughly the size of a walnut in its shell, and place them on the prepared trays, allowing them space to expand.

5. Bake for 12–14 minutes until golden brown but still soft in the middle. Remove from the oven and transfer the cookies, still on the baking parchment, to a wire rack to cool.

CHOCOLATE, MARMALADE, MANGO & PINE NUT TART

A chocolate tart with a secret surprise – the beautiful marmalade, mango and pine nuts in this recipe are hidden away beneath the chocolate filling, just waiting to show themselves when your serve up.

SERVES 8–10

1 x 26cm round Chocolate Sweetcrust Pastry case (see page 29)

150g marmalade

1 ripe mango, cut in half to remove the stone and the flesh thinly sliced and then cut away from the skin

50g pine nuts

Crème fraîche, to serve

FOR THE CHOCOLATE FILLING

125g unsalted butter, softened

125g caster sugar

2 eggs, lightly beaten

100g ground almonds

25g plain flour

25g cocoa powder

EQUIPMENT

Food processor or electric hand mixer

1. Make the Chocolate Sweetcrust Pastry case, remove it from the oven and keep the oven temperature at 170°C/Gas mark 3.

2. To make the chocolate filling, cream together the butter and sugar in the bowl of a food processor or with an electric hand mixer for about 5 minutes until they are light and fluffy. Add the eggs and ground almonds, and mix again until they are well combined. Sift the flour and cocoa powder over the mixture and stir in.

3. Spoon the marmalade into a small saucepan and heat gently just to warm and melt, so that it is easier to use. Spread the marmalade over the tart base and scatter the slices of mango over the top.

4. To finish, spread the chocolate mixture over the mango slices and sprinkle with the pine nuts. Bake for 15–20 minutes or until the filling is almost set, but still has a slight wobble. Serve warm or at room temperature with some crème fraîche.

CHOCOLATE TIFFIN

When we thought about recipes that could be put together in next to no time, the chocolate tiffin sprung to mind – a true Gü favourite. It involves no baking, just a bit of crushing, melting, mixing and leaving to set in the fridge. Fabulous!

MAKES ABOUT 16

300g digestive biscuits

125g unsalted butter

75g golden syrup

75g dark chocolate
(about 50% cocoa solids)

75g sultanas

100g dark chocolate (about 70% cocoa solids), melted (see page 10, or for tempered chocolate, see page 193)

FOR THE CARAMEL LAYER

1 tbsp liquid glucose or runny honey

100g caster sugar

150ml double cream

25g unsalted butter

Pinch of sea salt

EQUIPMENT

15 x 24cm baking tin

1. Line the baking tin with baking parchment. Drop half the biscuits into a plastic bag and bash with a rolling pin to create fine crumbs and then tip them into a large bowl. Break the remaining biscuits into small pieces with your hands and add to the bowl.

2. Gently melt the butter, golden syrup and the 75g dark chocolate for the base in a small saucepan. Pour over the biscuits and stir in with the sultanas. Spread the mixture evenly into the baking tin and place in the fridge.

3. To make the caramel layer, warm the glucose or honey in a high-sided pan and stir in the sugar with 1 teaspoon of water. Heat gently for 3–4 minutes without stirring until the sugar has dissolved and turned a golden brown colour.

4. Warm the cream in another saucepan and set aside. Remove the pan of caramel from the heat and, protecting your hands as it may splutter, gradually and very carefully stir one third of the warm cream into the caramel. Mix together and then stir in the remaining cream.

5. Stir in the butter and salt and bring the mixture back to the boil before removing the pan from the heat. Leave the caramel to cool then pour it evenly over the biscuit base. Place in the fridge to set.

6. Spread the melted chocolate over the set caramel. Place it back in the fridge to harden, then cut into pieces. If you have opted for a tempered chocolate topping, score the chocolate into fingers before it has fully set if you want to avoid cracking it.

GÜ TIP How about using ginger biscuits instead of digestives in the base for some added pizzazz?

COLATE
ESECAKE

This American-style baked cheesecake is a perfect dessert combination – a velvety cream cheese topping sitting over a crunchy chocolate biscuit base.

SERVES 8–10

150g digestive biscuits

2 tbsp cocoa powder

75g unsalted butter, melted

125g dark chocolate (about 70% cocoa solids), broken into small pieces

300ml whipping cream

350g full fat cream cheese

150g granulated sugar

1 egg, beaten

2 tbsp cornflour

EQUIPMENT

Food processor (optional)

18cm round springform cake tin

Electric hand mixer

1. Preheat the oven to 130°C/Gas mark ½. If you want to use your food processor (and who wouldn't?), tip the biscuits into the processor's bowl and blitz until they are finely crushed. Add the cocoa powder and mix well. Then, with the motor running, pour in the melted butter and mix just to combine.

2. For the harder workers among us, put the biscuits into a plastic bag and bash with a rolling pin. Add the cocoa powder and mix well. Tip the mixture into the saucepan of melted butter and mix just to combine.

3. With a spoon, press the biscuit mixture evenly into the base of the tin.

4. Put the chocolate pieces into a heatproof bowl. Pour the cream into a saucepan and bring it to the boil. Pour it over the chocolate and stir with a spatula until the chocolate has melted and become smooth.

5. Put the cream cheese with the sugar, egg and the cornflour into a large bowl and beat for 8–10 minutes with an electric hand mixer until you have a gloriously smooth mixture.

6. Fold the warm chocolate ganache into the beaten cheese mixture and spoon it onto the biscuit base, making sure that the surface is even.

7. Bake for 25–35 minutes or until the cheesecake is just starting to set around the edges, but is still wobbly in the centre. Remove from the oven, leave to cool and then chill in the fridge for at least a couple of hours if not overnight. Run a hot knife around the edge of the cheesecake before undoing the spring on the cake tin and serve cut into wedges.

GÜ TIP If you love amaretti biscuits, there's no reason why you couldn't use these for the base rather than digestive biscuits.

ROCKY ROAD

Rocky roads have become incredibly popular over the , years, so here's our version to tempt you. They are mouth watering nibbles that contain marshmallows and digestive biscuits smothered in chocolate and golden syrup.

MAKES 16

400g dark chocolate (about 70% cocoa solids), broken into small pieces

100g milk chocolate (34% minimum cocoa solids), broken into small pieces

75g unsalted butter

1½ tbsp golden syrup

6 digestive biscuits

50g mini marshmallows

50g sultanas

25g puffed rice

EQUIPMENT

20cm square baking tin

1. Put 300g of the dark chocolate and all of the milk chocolate into a heatproof bowl. Melt the butter and golden syrup in a small saucepan, then pour over the chocolate and stir with a spatula until the chocolate has melted and become smooth.

2. Break the digestive biscuits into pieces and drop them into the chocolate mix together with the marshmallows, sultanas and puffed rice. Stir well and spread evenly in the baking tin. Place in the fridge for a couple of hours to set.

3. Melt the remaining chocolate for the topping (see page 10, or if you want to temper the chocolate, see page 193) and spread it over the set biscuit base. Place it back in the fridge to harden, then cut into pieces. If you have opted for a tempered chocolate topping, score the chocolate into squares before it has fully set if you want to avoid cracking it.

GÜ TIP   To make a rocky road pud, tip the mixture onto a large 30cm long piece of cling film and roll it up like a sausage, twisting the ends to seal. Leave to set then brush it all over with melted chocolate and slice at the table. For added sharpness, crumble in 15g of freeze-dried raspberries at the same time as the puffed rice.

DARK ~~ƆLATE~~ ~~CAKE~~

Give in to happiness: bake this richest, most fudgy and gü-ey of chocolate cakes, dust it with cocoa powder and see the look on your friends' faces when you bring these slices of chocolate heaven to the table.

SERVES 12

150g dark chocolate (about 70% cocoa solids), broken into small pieces

100g dark chocolate (about 50% cocoa solids), broken into small pieces

250g unsalted butter, diced

300g light soft brown sugar

6 eggs, separated

Pinch of salt

Cocoa powder, for dusting

Single cream or crème fraîche, to serve

EQUIPMENT

23cm round springform cake tin

Electric hand mixer

1. Preheat the oven to 170°C/Gas mark 3 and butter and line the cake tin with baking parchment.

2. Put the chocolate into a heatproof bowl and add the butter. Tip the sugar into a small saucepan, add 4 tablespoons of water and bring to the boil, stirring to dissolve the sugar. Pour the mixture over the chocolate and butter and stir with a spatula until the chocolate and butter have melted and become smooth. Beat the egg yolks lightly with a fork and stir well through the chocolate mixture.

3. Whisk the egg whites and salt with an electric hand mixer in a bowl until they form soft peaks. With a metal spoon, mix one third of the whisked egg whites into the chocolate mixture, then gently fold in the rest.

4. Pour into the prepared tin and bake for about 50 minutes until a crust has formed and is starting to crack, but the cake is still soft in the centre and when a skewer is inserted in the centre it comes out clean. Remove from the oven and leave to cool in the tin. This wonderful fudgy cake is best served at room temperature or chilled overnight. Dust it with cocoa powder and serve with some runny single cream or crème fraîche.

GÜ TIP As if this cake isn't already delicious enough, go the full mile and drop small cubes of crystallised ginger into the surface of the cake just before baking, or stir in some finely grated orange zest or a pinch of ground star anise with the egg yolks.

... *for* **TREATS**

WARM CHOCOLATE MOUSSE

WITH COFFEE ICE CREAM

Light, airy and deliciously smooth, this pud is the perfect combination of a signature Gü chocolatey hot mousse served with a scoop of cold coffee ice cream.

SERVES 6

FOR THE COFFEE ICE CREAM

150g coffee beans

1 litre whole milk

2 egg yolks

250g caster sugar

300ml whipping cream

FOR THE WARM CHOCOLATE MOUSSE

2 tbsp whipping cream

125g dark chocolate (about 70% cocoa solids), melted (see page 10)

3 egg yolks

7 egg whites

1 tbsp granulated sugar

EQUIPMENT

Ice-cream maker or food processor

Electric hand mixer

6 x 200ml heatproof ramekins

1. To make the ice cream, preheat the oven to 140°C/Gas mark 1. Tip the coffee beans onto a baking tray and roast in the oven for about 20 minutes. Savour the aroma.

2. Pour the milk into a bowl and drop in the hot beans. Cover and leave to infuse for at least a couple of hours or overnight if possible.

3. Whisk the egg yolks with the sugar in a large bowl. Strain the coffee beans and pour the resulting milk into a saucepan with the cream. Bring to the boil, then pour the coffee cream onto the egg and sugar mix, whisking continuously.

4. Pour the mixture back into the cleaned pan and heat gently for about 5 minutes, stirring all the time. This is to cook the eggs and the mixture will only thicken very slightly. Remove the pan from the heat and pour its contents into a bowl. Place a piece of cling film on the surface of the custard to prevent a skin from forming, then leave to cool before chilling in the fridge.

5. Pour the custard into an ice-cream maker and churn to freeze. Alternatively, pour it into a plastic container and put it in the freezer, whisking well by hand every 30 minutes or so, until evenly slushy, then blitz it in a food processor. Return to the freezer for a further 30 minutes then blitz once more until smooth. Now freeze until set.

6. When ready to serve the mousse, remove the ice cream from the freezer to soften and preheat the oven to 180°C/Gas mark 4.

7. Put the cream in a small saucepan and bring it to the boil. Pour it over the melted chocolate and stir with a spatula until the chocolate has become smooth. Then stir in the egg yolks until well mixed.

recipe continues ...

8. Whisk the egg whites with an electric hand mixer in a bowl until they form soft peaks, then gradually whisk in the sugar until the mixture resembles shaving foam. With a metal spoon, mix one third of the whisked egg whites into the chocolate mixture, then gently fold in the rest.

9. Divide the mixture between the ramekins and bake for 4–5 minutes until the mousses are puffed up but still wobbly. Serve immediately with a scoop of the coffee ice cream on top.

GÜ TIP   As much as we'd love to think you could make this pud in our ramekins, please don't. They can't repeatedly be put in the oven.

CHOCOLATE TRUFFLES

A versatile treat, you can serve these smooth and creamy truffles after dinner, keep them all to yourself in a secret stash or be generous and give some as a gift. They also make truly fabulous decorations for a glazed cake, such as the Easy Chocolate Mousse Cake (see page 169), for special occasions.

MAKES ABOUT 25

FOR THE TRUFFLES

175g dark chocolate (about 70% cocoa solids), broken into small pieces

200ml whipping cream

50g unsalted butter

A little cocoa powder, for rolling

TO COAT THE TRUFFLES

200g dark chocolate (about 70% cocoa solids), melted (see page 10)

1 quantity Citrus Dust (see page 38)

EQUIPMENT

Stick blender (optional)

1. To make the truffles, put the chocolate pieces into a heatproof bowl. Pour the cream into a saucepan and bring it to the boil. Pour it over the chocolate and stir with a spatula until the chocolate has melted and become smooth. (If you have a stick blender, then use this to blitz the mixture to make it super smooth.)

2. Leave to cool for about 15 minutes, or to room temperature, then pinch off pieces of butter and beat into the chocolate mixture until smooth. Pour the mixture into a bowl, cover and chill in the fridge for 4–5 hours (or overnight) until the mixture has completely set.

3. Use a teaspoon to scoop out small spoonfuls of the truffle mix onto a baking tray or plate. Place the truffles back in the fridge to set for 10–15 minutes. Dust the palm of your hand with a little cocoa powder and roll each piece into a neat ball. Place the truffles back in the fridge to set once more for 10–15 minutes.

4. To coat the truffles, let the melted chocolate cool slightly and then put some of it on your hands. Roll the truffles one by one in your hands and then put them onto some baking parchment. Leave them in the fridge to set and scatter over the citrus dust before serving.

MILK CHOCOLATE, ORANGE & CARDAMOM TRUFFLES

Creamy smooth and fragrant with a flavour of the Middle East, these won't stay on the table for long.

MAKES ABOUT 40

FOR THE TRUFFLES

250g milk chocolate (34% minimum cocoa solids), broken into small pieces

125ml double cream

1 tsp honey

Finely grated zest of 1 orange

12 green cardamom pods, seeds removed and ground

A little cocoa powder, for rolling

TO COAT THE TRUFFLES

3 tbsp Citrus Dust (see page 38) (optional)

100g milk chocolate (34% minimum cocoa solids), melted (see page 10)

EQUIPMENT

Stick blender (optional)

1. Put the milk chocolate pieces into a heatproof bowl. Pour the cream and honey into a small saucepan, add the orange zest and ground cardamom and bring to the boil. Pour the hot cream over the chocolate and stir it with a spatula until the chocolate has melted and become smooth. (If you have a stick blender, then use this to blitz the mixture to make it super smooth.)

2. Pour the mixture into a bowl, cover and set aside in the fridge for 4–5 hours (or overnight) or until the mixture has completely set.

3. Use a teaspoon to scoop out small spoonfuls of the truffle mix onto a baking tray or plate. Place the truffles in the fridge to set for 10–15 minutes. Dust the palm of your hand with a little cocoa powder and roll each piece into a neat ball. Place the truffles back in the fridge to set once more for 10–15 minutes.

4. To coat the truffles, tip the citrus dust, if using, onto a shallow plate. Let the melted chocolate cool slightly and then put some of it on your hands. Roll the truffles one by one in your hands and then roll them in the citrus dust until evenly coated (or just leave coated in the chocolate) – it's best to do this with two people. Leave them in the fridge to set.

WHITE CHOCOLATE & WASABI TRUFFLES

Wasabi is a fiery horseradish from Japan, so you need to use it in moderation. These truffles are an unusual blend of creamy, sweet white chocolate with a hint of the hot hit of wasabi. Get your friends to guess the flavours.

MAKES ABOUT 40

FOR THE TRUFFLES

250g white chocolate, melted (see page 10)

125ml double cream

½–¾ tsp wasabi powder

1½ tsp honey

A little icing sugar, for rolling

TO COAT THE TRUFFLES

75g desiccated coconut

100g white chocolate, melted (see page 10)

EQUIPMENT

Stick blender (optional)

1. Put the chocolate pieces into a heatproof bowl. Pour the cream into a saucepan, bring to the boil and then stir in the wasabi powder and honey. Pour the hot cream over the chocolate and stir it with a spatula until the chocolate has melted and become smooth. (If you have a stick blender, then use this to blitz the mixture to make it super smooth.)

2. Pour the mixture into a bowl, cover and chill in the fridge for 4–5 hours (or overnight) until the mixture has completely set.

3. Use a teaspoon to scoop out small spoonfuls of the truffle mix onto a baking tray or plate. Place the truffles back in the fridge to set for 10–15 minutes. Dust the palm of your hands with a little icing sugar and roll each piece into a neat ball. Place the truffles back in the fridge to set once more for 10–15 minutes.

4. To coat the truffles, tip the desiccated coconut onto a shallow plate. Let the melted chocolate cool slightly and then put some of it on your hands. Roll the truffles one by one in your hands and then roll them in the desiccated coconut until evenly coated – it's best to do this with two people. Leave them in the fridge to set.

GÜ TIP Roll these chocs in toasted sesame seeds instead of the desiccated coconut.

VIENNESE BISCUITS

These elegant biscuits (traditionally called sablés Viennois – doesn't that sound romantic?) are similar to shortbread. The addition of egg white helps the biscuits to retain their pretty classic fluted shape during baking and gives added chewiness to the texture.

MAKES ABOUT 24

225g unsalted butter, softened

¼ tsp vanilla extract

150g golden icing sugar

250g plain flour

Pinch of salt

1 egg white

100g dark chocolate (about 70% cocoa solids)

EQUIPMENT

Piping bag fitted with a size 16 fluted piping nozzle

1. Beat the butter with the vanilla until it is soft and creamy, then beat in the icing sugar, flour, salt and egg white until smooth.

2. Preheat the oven to 170°C/Gas mark 3 and line two baking trays with baking parchment. Spoon some of the mixture into the piping bag fitted with the nozzle (be careful not to overfill as it will be tricky to pipe out) and pipe 24 equal-sized long biscuits onto the lined trays, allowing room for them to spread slightly. Top up the bag as necessary.

3. Bake for 10–12 minutes or until very lightly golden around the edges. Remove from the oven and leave them on the tray for about 5 minutes before transferring to a wire rack to cool completely.

4. Melt the chocolate (see page 10) and dip each end of the biscuits into it, shaking off any excess. Lay them on the prepared baking trays. Place the trays briefly in the fridge for the chocolate to set completely (if you don't do this, the biscuits are quite likely to go soggy). Serve with Chocolate Praline Spread or Gü Chocolate Ganache (see pages 52 and 30) in our glass ramekins to dip them into.

GÜ TIP Add some finely chopped pistachio or hazelnuts to the mix or add a pinch of ground spice such as cardamom, cinnamon or coriander (but make sure that you leave out the vanilla if using a spice otherwise the flavours will clash).

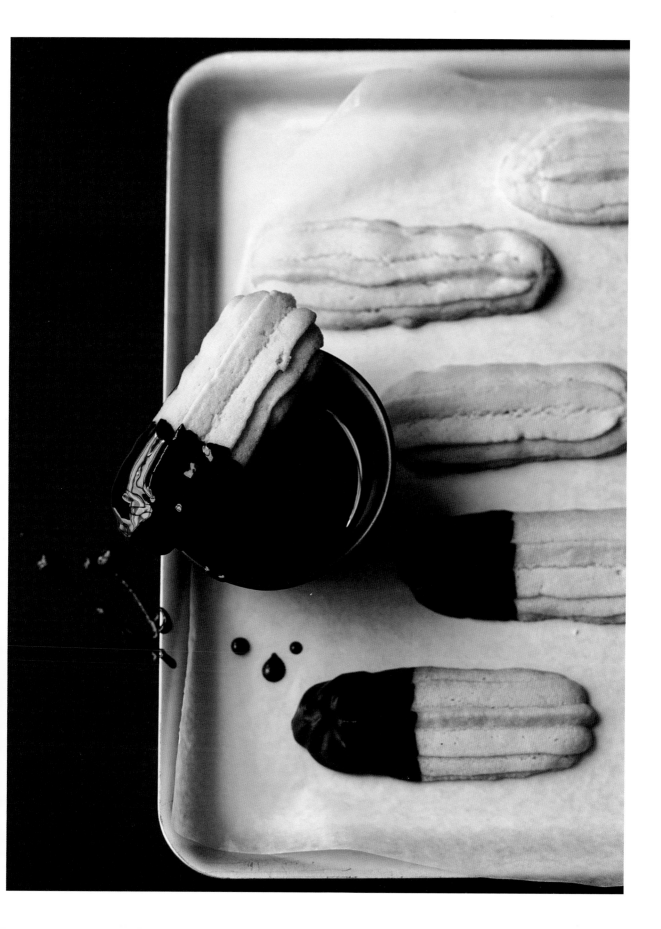

CHOCOLATE MADELEINES

Serve these scalloped little sponges when they are freshly made, and with some melted chocolate or warm Gü Chocolate Ganache (see page 30) on the side. They originate from northern France and are made with a light batter rather than the usual sponge cake mixture you might expect. You can buy special madeleine-shaped baking tins from any good bakery store or website for a truly authentic creation.

MAKES ABOUT 24

150g unsalted butter

115g plain flour

2 tbsp cocoa powder

2 tsp baking powder

2 eggs

90g caster sugar

1½ tbsp runny honey

3 tbsp milk

EQUIPMENT

12-cup madeleine tin

1. Melt the butter in a small saucepan, then remove it from the heat and set aside.

2. Sift the flour, cocoa powder and baking powder into a bowl. Beat the eggs, sugar and the honey together in another bowl and fold into the flour mix.

3. Pour the milk into a jug and pour in the melted butter. Stir the milk and butter into the batter, then cover and leave to chill in the fridge for at least an hour. (The madeleine mixture needs to be cold and the oven hot to obtain the domed effect so classic of madeleines, so if you can leave the batter overnight, even better.)

4. Preheat the oven to 170°C/Gas mark 3. Lightly butter the moulds in the madeleine tin, then dust them with flour, knocking out any excess.

5. Using a spoon, divide half of the mixture between the holes in the prepared tin and bake for 7–9 minutes or until risen and just cooked. To test, gently press the top of the madeleines and if the mixture bounces back, they are ready. Leave for 5 minutes in the tin, then turn out onto a wire rack to cool.

6. Clean the madeleine mould, then butter and flour again and repeat with the remaining mixture.

GÜ TIP For a hint of spice, grind the seeds of 6–8 green cardamom pods or take a pinch of ground star anise and stir them in with the milk and butter together with a small handful of chopped pistachios. Some finely grated orange zest or coffee powder stirred into the batter are great additions too.

CHOCOLATE CARAMELS

These smooth and chewy caramels are the perfect homemade pressie if you can bear to give them away. Pop the gorgeous little no-bake nibbles in a pretty box, wrap it up with a ribbon and you're good to go.

MAKES ABOUT 36

100g salted butter, softened

180ml double cream

240g caster sugar

80g liquid glucose or runny honey

50g dark chocolate (about 70% cocoa solids), broken into small pieces

EQUIPMENT

15 x 20cm or 18cm square baking tin

Sugar thermometer (optional)

1. Butter the baking tin evenly all over. Then lay a strip of baking parchment as wide as the tin in the base and up the sides, overlapping the top edge as this will help to lift the caramel from the tin once it has set.

2. Place the butter and cream in a small pan and heat gently until the butter has melted, then set aside.

3. Tip the sugar into a saucepan and add the glucose or honey together with 3 tablespoons of water. Place the pan over a medium heat and bring it to the boil, stirring continuously, until the sugar has dissolved. Then reduce the heat and let the contents continue to bubble gently (do not stir now) until the mixture turns a light caramel colour.

4. Keep an eye on the caramel, as you don't want it to catch and burn, but while it's cooking, melt the chocolate (see page 10).

5. When the sugar syrup has reached a light caramel colour, remove the pan from the heat and stir in the butter and cream mixture. Return the pan to the boil, then reduce the heat once again and simmer until it reaches 117–120°C (this is known as the soft-ball stage; see page 14 for checking that this has been reached, especially if you don't have a sugar thermometer). Remove the pan from the heat and stir in the melted chocolate until well mixed and smooth.

6. Pour the chocolate caramel into the prepared tin and leave it to set at room temperature. Using a knife, score into small diamond shapes, then cover and put in the fridge to set completely. To serve, remove the caramel from the tin, using the paper, and cut along the score lines.

CARAMELISED BANANA SPLIT

WITH WARM RUM CHOCOLATE GANACHE

Caramelised bananas, warm rum ganache, tasty popcorn, Chantilly cream and vanilla ice cream – all in all, a mind-blowing grown-up version of a children's classic.

SERVES 4–6

1 quantity Caramelised Popcorn or Puffed Rice (see page 34)

1 quantity Chantilly Cream (see page 20)

100g dark chocolate (about 70% cocoa solids), broken into small pieces

50g milk chocolate (34% minimum cocoa solids), broken into small pieces

150ml whipping cream

1 tbsp dark rum

3 small bananas

50g caster sugar

25g unsalted butter

Frozen plain yogurt or vanilla ice cream, to serve

1. Make the caramelised popcorn and leave to cool, and then make the Chantilly cream.

2. For the warm rum chocolate ganache, put the chocolate pieces into a heatproof bowl. Pour the cream into a saucepan and bring it to the boil. Pour it over the chocolate and stir with a spatula until the chocolate has melted and become smooth. Leave to cool a little, then stir in the rum.

3. For the bananas, line a baking tray with baking parchment, then cut the bananas lengthways in their skins. This helps to keep the bananas whole and looks great, too.

4. To make the caramel, tip the sugar into a large heavy-based frying pan and add 1 teaspoon of water. Heat gently for 3–4 minutes without stirring until the sugar has dissolved and turned a golden brown colour. Stir in the butter and then add the bananas, flesh-side down. Cook for about 5 minutes over a low heat until the bananas are golden. Carefully slide the bananas onto the prepared tray and leave for a few minutes to ensure that the caramel sets a little on the bananas.

5. Serve the banana halves in their skin with a scoop of frozen yogurt or vanilla ice cream. Top with a spoonful of Chantilly cream, sprinkle with some caramelised popcorn or puffed rice and serve the warm rum chocolate ganache on the side.

GÜ TIP In place of the popcorn, try some of our Caramelised Nuts instead (see page 37).

BROWNIE FINGERS

Here they are – brownies with a difference; in fact, they are double chocolate brownies as the fingers are topped with a chocolate glaze. For further yumminess, sprinkle the fingers with finely chopped crystallised ginger, or a mix of sunflower and pumpkin seeds or toasted pine nuts in place of the hazelnuts (in which case just toast 100g of the hazelnuts for the brownie mixture).

MAKES ABOUT 24

FOR THE BROWNIES

150g skinned hazelnuts

175g unsalted butter

150g dark chocolate (about 70% cocoa solids), broken into pieces

3 eggs

150g caster sugar

100g plain flour

¼ tsp salt

FOR THE GLAZE

250g dark chocolate (about 50% cocoa solids), broken into small pieces

200ml whipping cream

50g unsalted butter, diced

EQUIPMENT

16 x 25cm baking tin

1. Preheat the oven to 190°C/Gas mark 5 and butter and line the baking tin with baking parchment.

2. Tip the hazelnuts onto a baking tray and toast them in the oven for 6–8 minutes or until golden. Remove the nuts from the oven and leave to cool. Reduce the oven temperature to 170°C/Gas mark 3. Roughly chop the nuts, then set aside two thirds of them for the brownies and finely chop the rest to decorate.

3. Scrape the butter into a saucepan, drop in the chocolate pieces and melt gently, stirring until they have melted and become smooth.

4. Whisk the eggs and sugar together in a large bowl for a few minutes, then stir in the chocolate mixture. Sift the flour over the top, then add the salt and the roughly chopped hazelnuts, and mix well.

5. Scrape the mixture into the lined tin, level the surface and bake for 12–15 minutes or until the surface is dry but the middle still fudgy. Remove from the oven and leave to stand in the tin for 5 minutes, then turn out onto a wire rack and leave to cool. Cut the brownie into thin 7 x 2cm fingers, then lay them, bottom-side up, on the wire rack with space in between.

6. For the glaze, put the chocolate pieces into a heatproof bowl. Pour the cream into a saucepan and bring it to the boil. Pour it over the chocolate and stir with a spatula until the chocolate has melted and become smooth. Then beat in the butter, a cube at a time, until it is well incorporated.

7. Using a teaspoon, pour the chocolate glaze over each finger encouraging it to drip down the sides, then tap the rack to remove excess glaze. Sprinkle all the fingers with the finely chopped hazelnuts and place in the fridge to set.

GÜ TIP Don't forget about the hazelnuts when they are in the oven as toasted nuts can all too quickly turn into burned nuts.

CHOCOLATE RICE PUDDING

By adding the liquid a little at a time, this chocolatey rice pudding ends up with a wonderful creamy texture. Served with a moat of cream and sprinkled with chopped chocolate, it's just delectable.

SERVES 2

400ml whole milk

1½ tbsp whipping cream, plus 2 tbsp, to serve

30g caster sugar

1 vanilla pod

40g risotto rice

50g dark chocolate (about 70% cocoa solids), chopped, plus extra, to serve

1. Pour the milk and the cream into a saucepan and add the sugar. Split the vanilla pod lengthways and scrape out the tiny seeds that lay down its middle. Put them into the milk and cream mix and then drop in the pod. Bring to the boil, then remove from the heat, cover and leave for about 15 minutes to infuse.

2. Bring a small saucepan of water to the boil, add the rice and boil for a few seconds, then drain through a sieve and refresh with cold water immediately to cool it down.

3. Return the rice to the pan and add 2 tablespoons of the vanilla milk. Heat to a simmer and then, stirring all the time, add a ladleful of milk once the rice has absorbed the liquid.

4. Repeat the process until all the liquid has been absorbed. This takes 15–20 minutes and is ready once it's creamy and the rice is cooked. Finish by adding the 50g of chopped chocolate and mix until it is fully melted and incorporated. Serve the rice pudding warm or at room temperature (remembering to discard the vanilla pod), sprinkled with chopped chocolate and a spoonful of cream poured around it.

GÜ TIP Leave the rice pud to cool and serve with a spoonful of raspberry coulis (see page 110) stirred in, or some chopped toasted hazelnuts sprinkled over.

GÜ TIP Wash the used vanilla pod well and leave it to dry. Push this into a jar of sugar and after a week or two you'll have vanilla sugar to use in your cooking or stirred into coffee.

CHOCOLATE ICE CREAM LOLLIPOPS

What could be more fun than producing these tempting little lollipops on a lazy summery afternoon? The cocoa butter content in the chocolate will make the ice cream go very firm in the freezer after a few days so it is always better to consume a homemade ice cream as soon as you can – what a perfect excuse. If your lollipops are very hard, then leave them at room temperature for 5 minutes before handing out.

MAKES ABOUT 16

200g dark chocolate (about 70% cocoa solids), broken into small pieces

3 egg yolks

125g caster sugar

100ml whipping cream

500ml whole milk

2 tbsp liquid glucose or runny honey

FOR THE COATING

400g dark, milk or white chocolate, or a mixture of all three

TO DECORATE

Choose from:

Finely chopped nuts

Grated chocolate

Toasted seeds

Toasted coconut

EQUIPMENT

Sugar thermometer (optional, but helpful, see Gü technique, page 14)

Ice-cream maker or food processor

Small ice-cream scoop

16 lollipop sticks or wooden skewers

1. Put the chocolate pieces into a heatproof bowl and then beat the egg yolks and sugar together in another heatproof bowl.

2. Put the cream, milk and glucose or honey together in a saucepan and bring them to just below the boil. Pour two thirds of the hot mixture over the eggs and sugar, whisking all the time.

3. Pour the mixture back into the pan and place over a low heat. Cook gently, stirring all the time, until the mixture thickens slightly. (Don't let it get too hot or it will curdle.)

4. Pour the hot custard through a sieve over the chocolate and stir until it has melted and become smooth. Cover and chill in the fridge for a minimum of 4 hours for the flavour to mature.

5. Pour the chocolate custard into an ice-cream maker and churn to freeze. Alternatively, pour it into a plastic container and put it in the freezer, whisking well by hand every 30 minutes or so, until evenly slushy, then blitz it in a food processor. Return to the freezer for a further 30 minutes then blitz once more until smooth. Now freeze until set.

6. When the ice cream is set, line a baking tray (that will fit in your freezer) with baking parchment and use a small ice-cream scoop to transfer about 16 balls of the ice cream onto the prepared tray. Push a lollipop stick or wooden skewer into each ball. Put the tray in the freezer, and leave the ice cream to harden for a couple of hours.

7. Melt your chocolate of choice (see page 10) in a small but tall heatproof bowl or container. We suggest 'small but tall' as this makes it easier to dip and coat the ice cream.

recipe continues ...

8. Dip each lolly into the melted chocolate, rolling to cover and using a teaspoon to help bathe the lollies in the chocolate. Spin them to remove excess and then sprinkle over the decoration(s) of your choice. Return the lollies to the baking tray and then the freezer to harden.

GÜ TIP When making the custard, you could use a sugar thermometer to check its temperature, when it gets to 84°C it will be thickened enough and ready (for more tips for making the perfect custard, see page 13).

GÜ TIP You can flavour the ice cream by infusing spices, chilli or even citrus zest in the milk for a few minutes and then straining the milk to remove them.

GÜ CHOCOLATE MILKSHAKE

Here is a chocolate milkshake to beat all milkshakes – and it's not just for kids. Featuring our chocolate ganache, it is ultra decadent and delicious.

MAKES 4

200g dark chocolate (about 70% cocoa solids), broken into small pieces

200ml whipping cream

Vanilla ice cream

500ml milk

EQUIPMENT

Blender or smoothie maker

1. Put the chocolate pieces into a heatproof bowl. Pour the cream into a saucepan and bring it to the boil. Pour it over the chocolate and stir with a spatula until the chocolate has melted and become smooth.

2. Pour the chocolate mixture into ice-cube containers (silicone ones would be good) and freeze until solid.

3. For each milkshake, drop a quarter of the frozen chocolate cubes into a blender or smoothie maker with a large ball of ice cream and 125ml of the milk. Blend until smooth and serve straight away in a tall glass with a straw.

GÜ TIP To make a mocha shake, use Coffee Ice Cream (see page 90) instead of the vanilla ice cream or blitz in some orange marmalade or peanut butter for an extra kick.

TRIPLE CHOCOLATE COOKIES

No messing about here – this cookie recipe has the full-on chocolate hit with dark, milk and white chocolate chips liberally scattered throughout.

MAKES ABOUT 30

150g unsalted butter, softened
225g light soft brown sugar
1 egg, lightly beaten
1 tsp vanilla extract
225g plain flour
4 tbsp cocoa powder
½ tsp bicarbonate of soda
¾ tsp baking powder
Pinch of sea salt
150g dark chocolate chips
150g milk chocolate chips
150g white chocolate chips

EQUIPMENT
Food processor or electric hand mixer

1. Cream together the butter and sugar in the bowl of a food processor or with an electric hand mixer for about 5 minutes until they are light and fluffy. Add the egg and vanilla, and mix again until they are well combined.

2. Sift the flour, cocoa powder, bicarbonate of soda, baking powder and salt into a large bowl. Stir in the wet ingredients until just combined, then lightly knead in all the chocolate chips. Cover and put in the fridge for at least 24 hours.

3. If the dough is too hard to handle once it is chilled, leave at room temperature for 20–30 minutes to soften slightly. Preheat the oven to 170°C/Gas mark 3 and line a couple of baking trays with baking parchment.

4. Roll the cookie dough into about 30 evenly sized pieces, roughly the size of a walnut in its shell, and place them on the prepared trays, allowing them space to expand.

5. Bake for 12–14 minutes until golden brown but still soft in the middle. Remove from the oven and transfer the cookies, still on the baking parchment, to a wire rack to cool.

GÜ TIP Go one step further and turn these into Quadruple Chocolate Cookies by dipping half of each biscuit in the melted chocolate of your choice and leave to set.

RASPBERRY CHOCOLATE MOUSSE POTS

Perfect little shots of raspberry, brownie and mousse make for a brilliant combination of flavours and textures in these cute treats. To make life simpler, use a Gü chocolate brownie for this recipe, rather than going to the trouble of making your own – unless you have some homemade brownies just sitting there, of course (see page 72). For a real wow factor, make the impressive raspberry shards to decorate the top of the mousse. The rice flour included in the ingredients adds some extra crunch to the shards.

SERVES 6

½ chocolate brownie

100g dark chocolate (about 70% cocoa solids), broken into small pieces

100ml whipping cream

4 egg whites

25g caster sugar

FOR THE RASPBERRY SHARDS (OPTIONAL)

100g raspberries

1 tbsp rice flour

25g icing sugar

1 egg white

FOR THE RASPBERRY COULIS

150g fresh raspberries, plus extra, to serve

A splash of vodka (about ½ tbsp)

2–4 tbsp icing sugar

EQUIPMENT

Silicone mat (optional)

Food processor

6 pretty glasses

Electric hand mixer

6 drinking straws, to decorate (optional)

1. To make the raspberry shards, preheat the oven to 100°C/Gas mark ¼ and line a baking tray with a silicone mat or the matt side of some baking parchment. Put all the ingredients into a food processor and blitz until puréed. Pass the purée through a sieve to get rid of the seeds and then spread out thinly on the prepared tray. Bake for about 1 hour until the mixture has dried but still retains its red colour, then break into shards and store in an airtight container for up to a week. If they should become soft in that time, just place them back in the oven at the same temperature for about 10 minutes.

2. To make the raspberry coulis, tip the raspberries into a food processor and blitz until smooth. Scrape out into a bowl, then pour in the vodka and stir in the sugar to taste (raspberries always vary in sweetness). Pour into a sieve set over a bowl and push the sauce through with the back of a spoon to remove the seeds.

3. Divide the coulis between the serving glasses, then crumble some brownie over each.

4. Next make the chocolate mousse. Put the chocolate pieces into a heatproof bowl. Pour the cream into a saucepan and bring it to the boil. Pour it over the chocolate and stir with a spatula until the chocolate has melted and become smooth. Set aside.

5. Whisk the egg whites with an electric hand mixer in a bowl until they form soft peaks, then gradually whisk in the sugar until the mixture resembles shaving foam. With a spatula, mix one third of the whisked egg whites into the chocolate mixture, then gently fold in the rest.

6. Divide the chocolate mousse between the glasses and place in the fridge for a couple of hours. Drop a few raspberries into each glass, pop in a drinking straw to decorate, if using, and serve.

GÜ TIP Add about ¼ of a grated or deseeded and finely chopped red chilli to the raspberries when you blitz them for an extra hit.

MILLIONAIRE'S FLAPJACK

Why stick to just ordinary flapjacks when you can take them up a notch to these truly decadent chocolate delights? If you've got the time, make the flapjack mixture and leave it overnight before adding the topping. This will allow the oats to soften and make the flapjack chewier, which is just how it ought to be. Add a sprinkling of edible gold glitter if you are in the mood ...

MAKES 16

125g unsalted butter

50g light soft brown sugar

Pinch of salt

100g golden syrup

1 tbsp condensed milk

225g jumbo oats

100g dark chocolate (about 50% cocoa solids), broken into small pieces

FOR THE CARAMEL LAYER

75g light soft brown sugar

75g unsalted butter

200ml condensed milk

EQUIPMENT

16 x 25cm baking tin

1. For the flapjack base, tip the butter, sugar and salt into a pan. Add the golden syrup and condensed milk and gently heat to melt everything together.

2. Tip in the oats and mix well. Scrape the oaty mixture into the baking tin, spread out evenly, cover with cling film and put in the fridge to rest overnight if you have time.

3. Preheat the oven to 170°C/Gas mark 3 and bake the flapjack for 10–15 minutes or until just starting to go brown around the edges. Remove from the oven and set aside to cool.

4. To make the caramel layer, gently heat the sugar and butter in a saucepan, stirring until melted. Add the condensed milk and bring to the boil. Reduce the heat and simmer for 5–8 minutes, stirring continuously, until the filling has thickened slightly. Pour the caramel onto the flapjack base and give the tin a tap on the work surface to remove any air bubbles. Place in the fridge to set.

5. Melt the chocolate for the topping (see page 10) and spread it over the set caramel. Place it back in the fridge to harden, then cut into 16 squares and devour.

GÜ TIP If you like the chocolate to have more of a chocolatey crack when you bite it, then temper the chocolate for the topping (see page 193). Score the chocolate before it has fully set, otherwise it will crack and split.

GÜ TIP To alter the flavour and colour of the caramel, use a different sugar like dark soft brown sugar or molasses sugar. Either of these will give the flapjack a richer flavour. You could also add a small handful of dried fruit or toasted nuts to the oat base. And how about milk chocolate for the topping?

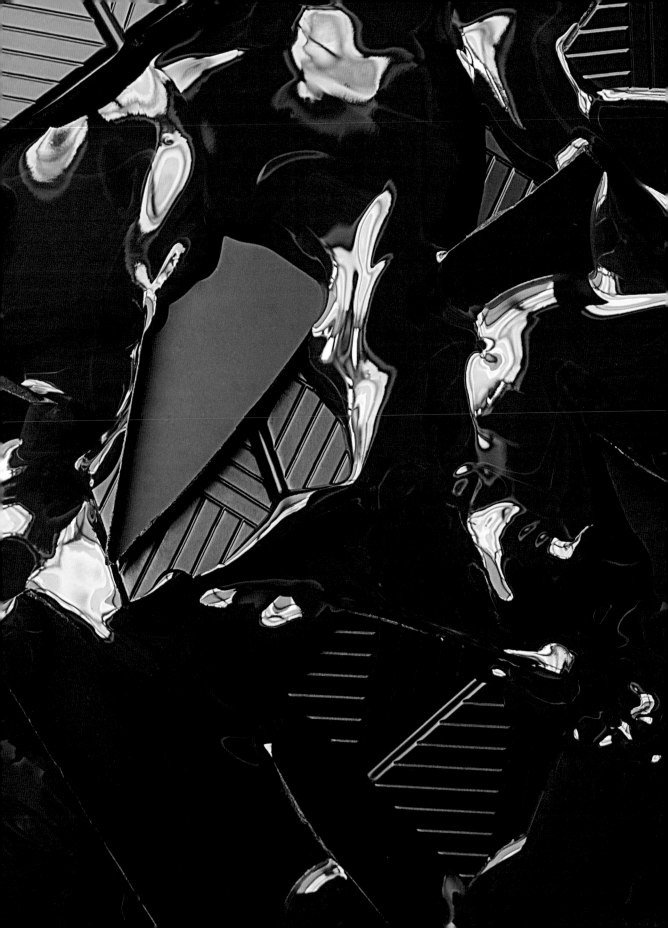

... *for* **FEEDING FRIENDS**

CHOCOLATE SOUP

WITH CARAMELISED BRIOCHE CROÛTONS

An unusual creamy sweet soup that is surprisingly fluffy and light. Brilliant for a dinner party dessert, it feels like such a special treat. Crème de cacao is a chocolate liqueur usually used as a base for cocktails. In this soup it gives an extra kick and really brings out the taste of the chocolate. For the ultimate finishing touch (but they are by no means obligatory), make gorgeous cubes of toasted brioche wrapped in crunchy caramel to sprinkle over the top.

SERVES 4

FOR THE CHOCOLATE SOUP

75g dark chocolate (about 50% cocoa solids), broken into small pieces

2 tbsp double cream

125ml milk

2 tsp crème de cacao (optional)

4 egg yolks

2 tsp caster sugar

Vanilla ice cream, to serve

FOR THE CARAMELISED BRIOCHE CROÛTONS (OPTIONAL)

1 small brioche bun or a thick slice of brioche loaf (about 50g total weight), cut into 2cm cubes

50g caster sugar

25g unsalted butter

EQUIPMENT

Electric hand mixer or free-standing mixer

1. For the chocolate soup, put the chocolate pieces into a heatproof bowl. Pour the cream and milk into a saucepan and bring to the boil. Pour it over the chocolate and stir with a spatula until the chocolate has melted and become smooth. Leave to cool, then stir in the crème de cacao, if using.

2. If you are making the caramelised brioche croûtons, preheat the oven to 160°C/Gas mark 3. Scatter the brioche cubes over a baking tray and toast in the oven for 5–10 minutes until lightly golden. Line another baking tray with baking parchment.

3. Tip the sugar into a saucepan and add 2 teaspoons of water. Heat gently for 3–4 minutes without stirring until the sugar has dissolved and turned a golden brown colour. Remove from the heat and carefully stir in the butter.

4. Add the toasted croûtons and turn to coat. Tip them out onto the lined tray, separating the pieces so they don't stick together. Leave to cool and harden.

5. Just before serving, whisk the egg yolks with an electric hand mixer or free-standing mixer for 5 minutes until they are light and fluffy.

6. Meanwhile, put the sugar into a small saucepan, add 2 teaspoons of water and bring to the boil, stirring to dissolve. Then, still using the hand or free-standing mixer, slowly pour the dissolved sugar over the egg yolks and whisk for a further 5 minutes.

7. Return the pan of chocolate to a low heat and stir in the whisked egg mixture. Heat gently for a minute or so. Pour the chocolate into soup bowls and place a scoop of ice cream in the centre. Serve straight away with the croûtons scattered over, if using.

GÜ TIP For simpler croûtons, dice the brioche bun or thick slice of brioche loaf as above, scatter on a baking tray and toast in the oven until lightly golden.

WHITE CHOCOLATE & COFFEE CRÈME BRÛLÉE

Under a warm and crunchy caramel layer hides a cool and creamy, delicately infused coffee custard just waiting to be discovered. Alternatively, you could leave out the coffee beans and drop a couple of raspberries into the cream just before baking or maybe top the plain brûlée with scooped-out passion fruit, instead of caramelising the tops. So have fun and play around!

MAKES 10

25g coffee beans

250ml whipping cream

250ml milk

100g white chocolate, finely chopped

6 egg yolks

50g caster sugar, plus extra, to sprinkle

EQUIPMENT

10 x 100ml ramekins or other ovenproof dishes

Sugar thermometer

Blow torch (optional)

1. Preheat the oven to 180°C/Gas mark 4 and set the ramekins in a baking tray. Tip the coffee beans onto a baking tray and roast in the oven for about 10 minutes to help release their flavour.

2. Pour the cream and milk into a saucepan, add the coffee beans and bring to the boil. Turn off the heat, cover the pan and leave to infuse for 20 minutes. Sieve to remove the beans and rinse out the saucepan.

3. Put the chocolate into a heatproof bowl.

4. Mix the egg yolks and sugar in a bowl. Pour in about 4 tablespoons of the coffee cream over the egg yolk mixture, whisking continuously, then pour over the rest of the coffee cream and whisk until smooth. Return to the rinsed saucepan and heat gently until the custard reaches 83°C on a sugar thermometer and coats the back of a spoon, taking care not to overheat the custard or it will split.

5. Remove from the heat and pour through a sieve onto the chocolate pieces. Leave for 1 minute and then gently mix well with a spatula.

6. Pour into the ramekins and place in the fridge for 4–5 hours (or preferably overnight) to chill completely.

7. Just before serving, preheat the grill to high and sprinkle the tops of the puddings very thinly and evenly with sugar. You only need a thin layer of sugar to get a crunchy layer, so don't be tempted to add more. Place under the grill and cook until the sugar has dissolved and turned a golden brown colour. Alternatively, use a blow torch to melt the tops. Let the caramel set (which only takes a few minutes) and serve.

GÜ TIP Our ramekins are not made to go repeatedly in the oven, so please don't use them for this recipe.

RASPBERRY GANACHE TART

Raspberries and chocolate are a classic combination, so that is what we've created here: a top of the class chocolatey and fruity tart to be shared with friends. Fabulous.

SERVES 8–10

1 x 20cm round Chocolate Sweetcrust Pastry case (see page 29)

FOR THE GANACHE FILLING

475g dark chocolate (about 70% cocoa solids), broken into small pieces

300ml whipping cream

1 tbsp honey

50g unsalted butter

300g raspberries

EQUIPMENT

Stick blender (optional)

1. Make the Chocolate Sweetcrust Pastry case. Once it has been blind baked, melt 75g of the chocolate (see page 10) and brush the inside of the pastry case to help stop it getting soggy too quickly.

2. For the ganache filling, put the remaining chocolate into a heatproof bowl. Pour the cream into a small saucepan, add the honey and bring it to the boil. Pour it over the chocolate and stir with a spatula until the chocolate has melted and become smooth. Leave to cool for about 5 minutes, then stir in the butter until it too has melted (using a stick blender here will make the filling even smoother).

3. Pour the ganache into the pastry shell, fill with a layer of raspberries and then place the tart in the fridge for a few hours or until set.

GÜ TIP For a nice surprise when you bite into the raspberries, why not add a little raspberry coulis into each raspberry (see page 110, made with or without the vodka), using a piping bag with the end snipped off.

GÜ TIP Sprinkle some Sesame Nougatine or thin shards of tempered chocolate (see pages 32 and 193) over the tart in place of the raspberries.

GÜ TIP For a mocha-flavoured ganache, reduce the whipping cream quantity to 275ml and add 25ml of espresso coffee in its place.

POT AU CHOCOLAT

Close friends of our best-selling Gü chocolate ganache, these silky smooth, chocolatey pots of gorgeousness really hit the spot. This recipe is incredibly easy to make, too, and can be prepared well in advance of dinner or your guests arriving for a party.

MAKES 10–12

4 egg yolks

1 tbsp caster sugar

½ tsp vanilla extract

200g dark chocolate (about 70% cocoa solids), broken into small pieces

400ml whipping cream

Pinch of sea salt

EQUIPMENT

10–12 x 100ml espresso cups or Gü ramekins

1. Place the egg yolks, sugar and vanilla extract in a heatproof bowl. Put the chocolate pieces into another heatproof bowl or large jug.

2. Pour the cream into a saucepan and add a pinch of salt then bring it to just below the boil. Pour it over the yolks and whisk lightly. Rinse out the saucepan with water. Pour the yolks and cream back into the rinsed saucepan and place over a low heat. Stir the custard until it lightly coats the back of a spoon.

3. Remove the pan from the heat and strain the custard through a sieve over the chocolate and leave for 1 minute. Gently stir until the chocolate pieces and warm custard are blended.

4. Pour the mixture evenly between the espresso cups or ramekins and chill in the fridge for at least 2 hours or overnight.

GÜ TIP Our ramekins are perfect for serving chilled puds.

GÜ TIP For a sexier version, add a tablespoon of rum, whisky or amaretto to the chocolate mixture before dividing it between the ramekins. Then, when it comes to serving, pour a tablespoon of cream on top, spoon on a dollop of Almond Chantilly Cream (see page 180) or sprinkle on some Chocolate Pecan Crumble (see page 31).

STIBLE
OLATE

OK – we're a bit biased, but we honestly think this is the most delicious chocolate tart ever invented. But we're not the only ones. A well-known celebrity chef asked us for the recipe, but rather than divulge our secret, we decided to share it with you in this book instead. The tart's melt-in-the-mouth, silky smooth texture and crumbly chocolate pastry make it an indulgent dessert which is surprisingly simple to make.

SERVES 8–10

1 x 26cm round Chocolate Sweetcrust Pastry case (see page 29)

FOR THE CHOCOLATE FILLING

280g dark chocolate (about 70% cocoa solids), broken into small pieces

230ml whipping cream

140ml milk

2 eggs

100g caster sugar

EQUIPMENT

Electric hand mixer or food mixer

1. Make the Chocolate Sweetcrust Pastry case, remove it from the oven and reduce the oven temperature to 110°C/Gas mark ¼.

2. To make the chocolate filling, put the chocolate pieces into a heatproof bowl. Pour the cream and milk into a saucepan and bring to the boil. Pour the creamy milk over the chocolate and stir with a spatula until the chocolate has melted and become smooth.

3. Put the eggs and sugar into a large heatproof bowl and place over a pan of simmering water. Whisk with an electric hand mixer for a few minutes, just enough to warm the mixture through.

4. Remove the bowl from the heat and continue whisking for 8–10 minutes or until it is very light and fluffy. This is known as a 'sabayon' and the more airy it is, the better (see page 13). With a spatula, fold one third of the sabayon into the chocolate mixture, then gently fold in the rest.

5. Pour the mixture evenly into the prepared tart shell, level the surface and bake for 9–11 minutes until just set but still wobbly. Leave it to cool, but don't be tempted to put the tart in the fridge as it really is best served at room temperature, when the texture is soft and melt in the mouth – totally irresistible. Well, we did warn you.

GÜ TIP Don't panic when you take the tart out of the oven and you think it looks like it hasn't set! The filling should be a soft, mousse-like consistency, not firm. Leave the tart for 2 hours at room temperature to firm up enough to slice.

GÜ TIP To make it easier to slice, cut the tart with a knife that you've dipped in hot water.

BOOZY CHERRY CHOCOLATE CLAFOUTIS

A clafoutis is a baked French dessert with a pancake-like batter covering fresh fruit, usually black cherries, although any variety is just as good – here's our chocolatey version. You might want to consider using blueberries or prunes that have been soaked in Armagnac for 30 minutes. Whichever you go with, the end result can be enjoyed warm or at room temperature. Such a versatile dessert.

SERVES 6–8

300g cherries, stoned
(see Gü technique, below)

2 tbsp Kirsch

100g caster sugar, plus 2 tbsp

15g unsalted butter, melted

2 tbsp demerara sugar

2 eggs

25g plain flour

100g dark chocolate (about 70% cocoa solids), broken into small pieces

300ml double cream

25g pistachios, chopped (optional)

Crème fraîche or vanilla ice cream, to serve

EQUIPMENT

24 x 19cm ovenproof dish

1. Drop the cherries into a bowl, then pour over the Kirsch and the 2 tablespoons of sugar. Toss together well and leave to macerate for a couple of hours.

2. Preheat the oven to 180°C/Gas mark 4. Brush the ovenproof dish with the melted butter and then sprinkle with the demerara sugar to evenly coat.

3. In a large bowl, beat the eggs and 100g caster sugar together. Sift the flour over the eggs and fold in until it's well incorporated.

4. Put the chocolate pieces into a heatproof bowl. Pour the cream into a saucepan and bring it to the boil. Pour it over the chocolate and stir with a spatula until the chocolate has melted and become smooth. Then stir the chocolate into the egg mixture until it is fully incorporated.

5. Tip the cherries with any resulting syrup into the mix, give it a good stir and then pour the mixture into the prepared dish. Bake for 25–35 minutes or until the top of the clafoutis domes slightly. Serve warm, sprinkled with pistachios, if using, and with crème fraîche or vanilla ice cream on the side – our glass ramekins would be the perfect containers.

GÜ TIP To stone your cherries, insert a cocktail stick into the stem end of the cherry and into the stone. Twist the cocktail stick around a little and you can then pop out the stone. To make the task a little less tedious, you might want to invest in a cherry stoner – you can use these for stoning olives, too.

GÜ TIP We think that the Chocolate Pecan Crumble (see page 31) sprinkled over the baked clafoutis is a luxurious additional topping.

CHOCOLATE FONDANT

Light and fluffy soufflé-like puds which can be made the night before and kept in the fridge. The next day, bring them back to room temperature before baking as described in the recipe. Simple.

MAKES 8

110g dark chocolate (about 70% cocoa solids), broken into small pieces

130ml whipping cream

2 whole eggs

4 egg yolks

60g caster sugar

Thick cream, Chantilly Cream (see page 20) or vanilla or chocolate ice cream, to serve

EQUIPMENT

8 x 200ml heatproof ramekins (remember that the Gü ramekins can't be reheated)

Electric hand mixer

1. Preheat the oven to 160°C/Gas mark 2 and set the ramekins in a baking tray. Put the chocolate pieces into a heatproof bowl. Pour the cream into a saucepan and bring it to the boil. Pour it over the chocolate and stir with a spatula until the chocolate has melted and become smooth.

2. Put the eggs, egg yolks and sugar into a large heatproof bowl and place over a pan of simmering water. Whisk with an electric hand mixer for a few minutes until just warmed through.

3. Remove the bowl from the heat and continue whisking for 8–10 minutes or until it is very light and fluffy. This is known as a sabayon and the more airy it is, the better (see page 13). With a spatula, fold one third of the sabayon into the chocolate mixture, then gently fold in the rest. Divide the mixture between the 8 ramekins, filling each one about three quarters full.

4. Bake in the oven for 10–12 minutes until just set but still a little wobbly. Remove the baking tray from the oven, take out the ramekins and serve them straight away. Drizzle with some thick cream, top with Chantilly cream or add a scoop of vanilla or chocolate ice cream to each one.

GÜ TIP To make Black Forest fondants, brush the inside of the ramekins with some melted butter. Scatter in some finely grated chocolate and turn to coat the insides, knocking out any excess. Continue the recipe as above but while the fondants are cooking, whip some cream with a splash of Kirsch to soft peaks. When the fondants are cooked, leave to cool for a couple of minutes, then gently press 2 or 3 cherries marinated in Kirsch (or fresh cherries) into the fondants. Spoon a little of the Kirsch Chantilly on top of each one and decorate with another cherry. Serve straight away.

CHOCOLATE & PEAR TARTE TATIN

It is said that the tarte tatin was created in 1889 in a French hotel by mistake when a pan of apples cooking in butter and sugar was burning. The chef, anxious to prevent a disaster, covered the apples with some pastry she was rolling out and popped it in the oven. Hey presto – a classic was born! We've swapped the apples for pears and, of course added some chocolate, and the end result is – dare we say it – close to perfection on a plate.

SERVES 6

100g caster sugar

50g unsalted butter, diced

25g dark chocolate (about 70% cocoa solids), finely chopped

3 large ripe pears (about 700g total weight), halved, cored and tossed in 1 tbsp lemon juice to stop them browning

250g ready-made puff pastry

Crème fraîche, to serve

EQUIPMENT

23cm frying pan with ovenproof handle or a 23cm round cake tin with a solid base

1. Preheat the oven to 190°C/Gas mark 5. To make a caramel sauce, tip the sugar into a saucepan and add 1 teaspoon of water. Heat gently for 3–4 minutes without stirring until the sugar has dissolved and turned a golden brown colour.

2. Remove the pan from the heat and stir in the butter. Then whisk in the chocolate, add a few drops of water and whisk again. Bring back to the boil and remove from the heat once more. Arrange the pear halves cut-side up around the frying pan. (If you are using a cake tin, pour the caramel into the tin and arrange the pears on top, again cut-side up.)

3. Lightly dust a work surface with flour and roll out the pastry to about 5cm larger than the pan or tin. Slide the pastry on top of the pears, tucking the edges down the inside of the container and bake in the oven for 20–25 minutes or until the pastry is crisp and golden. Leave to cool for 5 minutes before inverting onto a plate, fruit-side up. Serve this ever-popular pud while it is still warm and with some crème fraîche.

GÜ TIP Sprinkle the finished tarte tatin with Caramelised Nuts (see page 37) or finely chopped candied ginger, or add a pinch of cinnamon to some whipped cream to serve instead of the crème fraîche.

GÜ TIP You can make individual versions in small tart tins, or tiny ones made in mini muffin tins are fabulous nibbles.

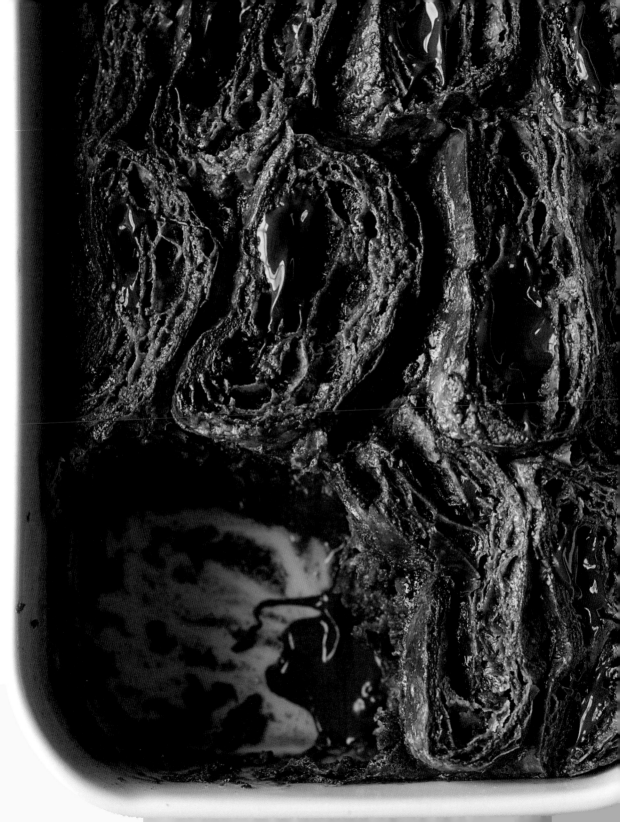

PAIN AU CHOCOLAT
BREAD & BUTTER PUDDING

This recipe is a great way to use up leftover pain au chocolat or croissants. In fact, it's actually better if they are a little stale because they absorb the custard better. Once cooked the pudding is crispy over the top and the edges, and it is smooth, rich and creamy on the inside.

SERVES 4–6

4 pain au chocolat

75ml milk

200ml whipping cream

75g dark chocolate (about 70% cocoa solids), broken into small pieces

50g caster sugar

2 eggs

Whipped cream or vanilla ice cream, to serve

EQUIPMENT

16 x 22cm ovenproof dish

1. Preheat the oven to 150°C/Gas mark 2. Cut each pain au chocolat into three equal pieces across widthways and pack them into the ovenproof dish.

2. Pour the milk and cream into a saucepan and bring to the boil. Drop in the chocolate and stir until it has melted and become smooth.

3. Mix the sugar and eggs together in a bowl and pour the chocolate mixture over, whisking all the time. Then slowly pour the custard over the pain au chocolat, allowing the custard to be absorbed before adding more.

4. Bake for 25–30 minutes or until the top is lightly crisp and the centre still wobbly. Serve warm with cream or ice cream.

GÜ TIP Stir a little finely grated orange zest or a handful of raisins soaked in a tablespoon of rum into the milk as it comes to the boil. For something a little more fruity, scatter some cherries, or diced poached pear (see page 56) among the pain au chocolat before pouring on the custard.

CHOCOLATE SOUFFLÉ

The Gü chocolate soufflé – our iconic first creation and still our top seller. Why not try making your own at home? While soufflés have the reputation of being tricky to make, in reality this isn't the case. However, we do recommend that you prepare the pots as suggested because this helps them to rise evenly. Ensure your ingredients are all at room temperature, too. You might think you can get away with butter, milk and eggs straight from the fridge, but no – you'd be wrong!

MAKES 6

250g dark chocolate (about 70% cocoa solids), broken into small pieces

25g unsalted butter, melted

300ml whole milk

2 tbsp cornflour

3 egg yolks, lightly beaten

5 egg whites

100g caster sugar

EQUIPMENT

6 x 200ml heatproof ramekins

Electric hand mixer

1. Preheat the oven to 190°C/Gas mark 5. Finely grate 50g of the chocolate and set aside. Brush the ramekins with the melted butter and then coat them with the grated chocolate, shaking out any excess.

2. Mix 4 tablespoons of the milk with the cornflour in a bowl until smooth and then whisk in the rest of the milk. Pour into a saucepan and bring the milk to the boil, whisking all the time, until it has thickened and is smooth.

3. Drop the chocolate pieces into the custard and whisk until they have melted and the custard is smooth. Leave to cool for 5 minutes then stir into the egg yolks.

4. Whisk the egg whites with an electric hand mixer in a bowl to soft peaks, then gradually whisk in the sugar until the mixture resembles shaving foam. With a metal spoon, mix one third of the whisked egg whites into the chocolate mixture, then gently fold in the rest.

5. Divide the mixture evenly between the ramekins, filling each to the very top. Level the surface and wipe around the rim of each ramekin with a finger to help the soufflés to rise straight. Bake for 8–12 minutes until risen and fluffy.

GÜ TIP The soufflé mixture can be made and kept in the fridge overnight before baking. You could freeze the mixture too, allowing it to defrost before dividing between the ramekins and baking as described in Step 5.

GÜ TIP Our ramekins can't be re-used in the oven, so keep them for other uses, such as serving up whipped cream or some truffles.

CHOCOLATE, FIG & PEAR TRIFLE

We've taken the liberty of including some Gü nibbles with this recipe; only to make it easier for you to make, of course. The Gü chocolate brownies are used in place of the more traditional sponge cake, although you could also use the Chocolate and Pecan Muffins or Gücpakes (minus their chocolate ganache frosting) recipes on pages 43 and 65.

SERVES 6–8

3 ripe pears (about 350g total weight)

Juice of 1 lemon

3 tbsp dark soft brown sugar

6 figs (about 150g total weight)

3 tbsp Marsala wine

240g Gü chocolate brownies, muffins or cupcakes (see the recipe introduction)

250g tub of mascarpone cheese

200g crème fraîche

2 tbsp caster sugar

½ tsp vanilla extract

2 egg yolks

75g dark chocolate (about 70% cocoa solids), finely grated

200ml whipping cream

25g toasted skinned hazelnuts, crushed

1. Preheat the oven to 180°C/Gas mark 4. Peel, core and chop the pears into small cubes and drop into a small baking dish with the lemon juice and dark soft brown sugar. Cut the figs into quarters and add to the dish with the Marsala wine and toss well.

2. Bake for 20–30 minutes or until the pears are tender. Remove them from the oven and set aside to cool.

3. Break whichever cake you're using – brownies, muffins or cupcakes – into chunks and drop into the base of a serving bowl. Spoon over the pears, figs and about half of the juices, reserving the rest.

4. Beat together the mascarpone cheese, crème fraîche, caster sugar, vanilla and egg yolks in a bowl until smooth and then stir in half of the chocolate. Spoon the mixture evenly over the pears and figs.

5. Whip the cream with the reserved pear and fig juices until it forms soft peaks and spoon over the trifle. Sprinkle with the crushed hazelnuts and remaining grated chocolate and place in the fridge until ready to serve.

MELT IN THE MIDDLE

Not only is this an absolutely gorgeous pudding with a melting centre, it's also very clever, as you can make and bake it the day before, refrigerate, then bring back to room temperature and reheat just before serving. This makes it particularly brilliant for dinner parties because it allows you to spend more time with your mates and less time in the kitchen.

MAKES 8

200g unsalted butter

200g dark chocolate (about 70% cocoa solids), broken into small pieces

6 eggs

240g caster sugar

60g plain flour

EQUIPMENT

8 x 200ml heatproof ramekins or 75–80mm diameter metal rings

Electric hand mixer

1. Preheat the oven to 180°C/Gas mark 4. If you are using the chef rings, lightly butter each ring and line with a piece of baking parchment that is large enough to go to the top of the mould.

2. Put the butter in a small saucepan and drop in the chocolate. Heat gently until the butter has melted, then remove the pan from the heat and stir it with a spatula until the chocolate has melted and become smooth.

3. Whisk the eggs and sugar together in a large bowl with an electric hand mixer until ribbon stage: when the beaters are lifted from the mixture, they leave a thin trail of the mixture on the surface. With a metal spoon, fold the chocolate mixture into the eggs and sugar and sift the flour over the top. Fold together well.

4. Divide the mixture between the ramekins or metal rings, filling each one three quarters full. Bake the ramekins for 8–10 minutes or metal rings for 6–7 minutes until a crust has started to form around the cakes, but the middle is still like a gü-ey pool of chocolate. To serve, turn the puddings out of the ramekins or metal rings and enjoy the look on everyone's faces as they tuck in.

GÜ TIP Crumble over some chopped nuts or Chocolate Pecan Crumble (see page 31) just before baking.

GÜ TIP These little puds can be baked in advance and then warmed up in a microwave oven. Heat them for 20–30 seconds at 800w and check that they are warm enough. If not, heat for 10 second blasts until they are just right.

GÜ TIP Gü ramekins are good for many things, but not for putting in a hot oven more than once. Please don't use them for this recipe.

STICKY CHOCOLATEY TOFFEE PUD

Here is a Gü take on a classic that never fails to please, especially on a dark winter's night. Light the fire, pull on your cosiest jumper, and get stuck into this sticky delight – with or without your friends.

SERVES 6–8

75g stoned dates

75g dried apricots

100g plain flour

1 tsp cornflour

1 tsp baking powder

½ tsp bicarbonate of soda

100g dark soft brown sugar

50g unsalted butter

1 egg, lightly beaten

Vanilla ice cream, to serve

FOR THE STICKY CHOCOLATEY TOFFEE SAUCE

350ml whipping cream

50g caster sugar

1 generous tsp black treacle

1 generous tbsp golden syrup

50g dark chocolate (about 50% cocoa solids), broken into small pieces

EQUIPMENT

Food processor

16 x 22cm ovenproof dish

1. Drop the dates and apricots into a small saucepan, pour over 125ml of water and bring it to the boil. Reduce the heat and simmer for 5–10 minutes or until the fruits are very tender and soft. Leave to cool slightly, then blitz in a food processor to a purée and set aside.

2. Preheat the oven to 170°C/Gas mark 3. Sift the flour with the cornflour, baking powder and bicarbonate of soda. Beat the dark soft brown sugar and butter together well until fluffy and gradually beat in the egg. Stir in the flour mix and then stir in the fruit purée.

3. Scrape the mix into the ovenproof dish and bake for 25–30 minutes or until when you touch the top, the mixture springs back.

4. Meanwhile, make the sticky toffee sauce. Pour 300ml of the cream into a saucepan and add the caster sugar, treacle and golden syrup. Bring to the boil, then reduce the heat and simmer until it has thickened and turned a light brown caramel colour.

5. Remove from the heat and stir in the chocolate pieces until they have melted and become smooth. Then stir in the remaining cream and serve warm with the pudding and ice cream.

GÜ TIP What could be tastier than a sprinkling of chopped and toasted pecans, walnuts, almonds, pistachios or brazil nuts on top for some added crunch.

CHOCOLATE MOUSSE

This classic French mousse recipe was handed down from our chef Fred's grandmother Julienne. He simply couldn't resist handing it on to you in this book.

MAKES 6

125g dark chocolate (about 70% cocoa solids), broken into small pieces, plus extra to decorate

75g dark chocolate (about 50% cocoa solids), broken into small pieces

125ml whipping cream

50ml milk

4 egg whites

25g caster sugar

EQUIPMENT

Electric hand mixer

6 glasses or Gü ramekins

1. Put the chocolate pieces into a heatproof bowl. Pour the cream and milk into a small saucepan and bring to the boil. Pour the creamy milk over the chocolate and stir with a spatula until the chocolate has melted and become smooth.

2. Whisk the egg whites with an electric hand mixer in a bowl until they form soft peaks, then gradually whisk in the sugar until the mixture resembles shaving foam. With a metal spoon, mix one third of the whisked egg whites into the chocolate mixture, then gently fold in the rest.

3. Divide the chocolate mousse between the glasses, cover and place in the fridge for 2–3 hours or until chilled and set. Grate over a little chocolate to decorate.

GÜ TIP There are some classic flavour combinations for dressing up chocolate mousse. Finely grate the zest of an orange into the milk before heating or finely chop a knob or two of stem ginger and stir this into the cream and milk mixture. A splash of amaretto stirred in would also be a delicious addition, or sprinkle over some Citrus Dust or crumbled Sesame Nougatine (see pages 38 and 32).

GÜ TIP For a mousse with a really surprising kick, use a Microplane grater (see page 16) to very finely grate a medium hot chilli into the milk before you heat it and then leave it to infuse in there. The longer you leave it, the hotter it will get, but about 15–20 minutes should do it. Then strain out the chilli. If you don't have a Microplane grater, then deseed it and chop it as finely as you can.

WHITE CHOCOLATE PARFAIT

WITH SALTED CARAMEL

The word *parfait* in French means 'perfect', and that's exactly how we feel about this little gem of a dessert. It's a simple frozen pud made of sugar syrup, eggs and cream – our version has a smooth caramel hiding beneath a creamy white chocolate topping.

MAKES 6

½ quantity Salted Caramel Sauce (see page 26)

4 egg yolks

100g caster sugar

50g white chocolate, broken into small pieces

250ml whipping cream

25g salted peanuts, crushed

EQUIPMENT

Sugar thermometer (optional)

Electric hand mixer (optional)

6 x 200ml freezerproof glass dishes

1. Make the salted caramel sauce and leave to chill.

2. For the parfait, whisk the egg yolks in a large bowl. Tip the sugar into a small saucepan and add 1 tablespoon of water. Heat gently for 3–4 minutes without stirring until the sugar has dissolved, then increase the temperature to medium and bring to the boil. Continue to heat the syrup until the sugar thermometer reads 117–120°C (this is known as the soft-ball stage; see page 14 for checking that this has been reached, especially if you don't have a sugar thermometer). Remove from the heat and pour the syrup into the yolks, whisking all the time with a hand whisk or electric hand mixer and continuing to do so until it starts to cool.

3. Melt the chocolate (see page 10) and whip the cream to soft peaks. Fold the melted chocolate into the sabayon and then fold in the whipped cream.

4. Divide the liquid caramel between the dishes and top with the parfait. Cover and freeze for 3–4 hours, but don't freeze for much longer than that or they will become rock hard. Remove the dishes from the freezer 2 minutes before serving and sprinkle with the crushed salted peanuts.

GÜ TIP Favourite flavours to add to the mix are cherries infused in Kirsch, crushed raspberries or diced mango mixed with passion fruit, or quite simply just some lime zest. It's your call.

TIRAMIGÜ

'Pick me up' is the direct Italian translation of tiramisu and this is sure to give your guests the chocolate hit they are looking for. To jazz up this simple tiramisu, we've added a quick recipe for making your own chocolate sponge fingers. You can, of course, use about 24 ready-made sponge fingers or savoiardi biscuits instead and it will be just as delectable. If this is the case, start at Step 4 of the method.

SERVES 6–8

100ml strong coffee for dipping

75g dark chocolate (about 70% cocoa solids), chopped

Cocoa powder, for dusting

FOR THE CHOCOLATE SPONGE FINGERS

50g plain flour

2 tbsp cocoa powder

3 egg whites

50g caster sugar

2 egg yolks, lightly beaten

FOR THE MASCARPONE MOUSSE

500g mascarpone cheese

75g caster sugar

1 egg yolk

2 tbsp coffee liqueur

200ml whipping cream

EQUIPMENT

25 x 30cm baking tray

Electric hand mixer

20cm square serving dish or 6–8 individual dishes

1. To make the sponge fingers, preheat the oven to 170°C/Gas mark 3 and line the baking tray with baking parchment.

2. Sift the flour and cocoa powder together in a bowl. Whisk the egg whites with an electric hand mixer in a bowl to soft peaks, then gradually whisk in the sugar until the mixture resembles shaving foam. With a metal spoon, fold in the egg yolks.

3. Carefully fold in the flour and cocoa powder and spread the mixture out gently and evenly onto the lined tray. Bake for 8–10 minutes or until when you press the surface gently with your finger the mixture bounces back. Leave to cool, then cut in half lengthways and cut across into 2cm-wide fingers.

4. To make the mascarpone mousse, tip the mascarpone, sugar, egg yolk, coffee liqueur and cream into a large bowl and beat with a spatula until the mixture forms soft peaks.

5. Pour the coffee into a shallow dish and dip half of the sponge fingers into this then lay them evenly into the base of the serving dish (or dishes).

6. Cover with half of the mascarpone mousse, spread evenly over the biscuits. Soak the remaining sponge fingers and layer them over the mousse before spreading the rest over the top. Sprinkle with the chopped chocolate and dust with a little cocoa powder.

GÜ (EVEN MORE CHOCOLATEY) TIP   If you have the time and a full chocolate addiction (we do), replace the grated chocolate and cocoa finishing touches with some Gü Chocolate Ganache (see page 30).

CHOCOLATE MARTINI

A martini is traditionally made with gin and vermouth, garnished with a twist of lemon or an olive. We've taken this one step further by introducing – yes! – a chocolate liqueur together with an added hit of grated chocolate or a chocolate button. It's always a favourite at a Gü party.

MAKES 4

2 squares of chocolate
or 4 chocolate buttons

Plenty of ice cubes

160ml crème de cacao

160ml vodka

EQUIPMENT

Cocktail shaker

4 martini glasses

1. If you are using squares of chocolate rather than chocolate buttons, grate the chocolate onto a plate and place in the fridge.

2. Crush some ice (try putting the ice cubes in a clean tea towel and bashing them with a rolling pin) and tip into a large jug or cocktail shaker. Pour over the crème de cacao and vodka, cover with a tea towel or lid, and shake well – unless your preference is for a stirred martini.

3. Pour the cocktail mixture, leaving the ice behind, into the glasses and sprinkle with the grated chocolate or drop in a chocolate button. Serve immediately. Drink and repeat!

WHITE CHOCOLATE ETON MESS

Our French chef Fred has learned to love so many English puddings and none less than Eton mess. He particularly likes the idea of a big summer lunch with huge meringues, which can be bashed up by kids using a rolling pin. If time is short, you could always use shop-bought meringues and not worry about making the strawberry syrup. While the end result wouldn't be quite the same, it would still be pretty darned pleasing.

SERVES 4–6

5 egg whites

150g caster sugar

150g icing sugar

300g strawberries, to serve

FOR THE WHITE CHOCOLATE CHANTILLY

100g white chocolate, broken into small pieces

275ml whipping cream

1 tbsp glucose or runny honey

FOR THE STRAWBERRY SYRUP

300g strawberries, hulled and cut in half

25g caster sugar

FOR THE MINT SUGAR

50g caster sugar

Mint leaves

EQUIPMENT

Electric hand mixer

1. To make the Chantilly cream, put the chocolate pieces into a heatproof bowl. Put 75ml of the cream and the glucose or honey into a small saucepan and bring to the boil. Pour the mixture over the chocolate and stir with a spatula until the chocolate has melted and become smooth. Stir in the remaining cream, and place in the fridge for 3–4 hours to crystallise.

2. To make the meringues, preheat the oven to 110°C/Gas mark ¼ and line a baking tray with baking parchment. Whisk the egg whites with an electric hand mixer in a bowl to soft peaks, then gradually whisk in the caster sugar until the mixture resembles shaving foam. Then carefully fold in the icing sugar.

3. Spoon the meringue on the prepared tray in a big dollop and bake for 50–60 minutes or until the meringue is crunchy and dry, but light and airy in the middle. Keep in an airtight container.

4. For the strawberry syrup, tip the strawberries and sugar into a heatproof bowl and cover with cling film. Bring a pan of water to a simmer over a low heat, place the bowl over it and simmer for an hour, checking occasionally to make sure that the pan doesn't dry out. Remove it from the heat and leave the syrup to cool.

5. Tip the strawberries into a fine sieve and leave to drain. Don't press the strawberries because you want to keep the juice clear. Discard the cooked pieces of strawberry and put the juice in the fridge to chill.

6. Make the mint sugar, crush the sugar and mint leaves together in a mortar with the pestle until the two have blended together.

7. To create this particularly magnificent Eton mess, whip the Chantilly cream until it forms soft peaks. Break the meringue into the cream. Prep your remaining strawberries, gently mix everything together and serve. Let your guests drizzle the strawberry juice and sprinkle the mint sugar over the top as they see fit.

RABBIT RAGÜ

WITH WHITE CHOCOLATE AND PARSNIP PURÉE

Rabbit, white chocolate and parsnip may strike you as an unusual combination, but it really is very good so your friends and family will be begging you for the recipe at the end of the meal.

SERVES 4

2 tbsp vegetable or olive oil

800g–1kg rabbit or chicken, cut into 8 pieces, with bone

150g pancetta, cut into small strips

200g mushrooms, quartered if large

1 onion, peeled and chopped

Sprig of thyme

1 garlic clove, peeled and crushed

1 tbsp plain flour

200ml white wine

400ml hot vegetable or chicken stock

75ml whipping cream

Splash of lemon juice

Salt and freshly ground black pepper

Small bunch of flat-leaf parsley, chopped

FOR THE PARSNIP PURÉE

4 parsnips (about 800g total weight), peeled and cut into even-sized pieces

100g white chocolate, broken into small pieces

100ml whipping cream

1. Heat the oil in a large heavy-based pan or casserole over a medium heat. Add the rabbit pieces and brown them on all sides. Remove the rabbit pieces from the pan with a slotted spoon and set aside.

2. Add the pancetta, mushrooms, onion, thyme and garlic to the pan and cook, stirring occasionally, until golden brown.

3. Return the rabbit pieces to the pan and sprinkle with the flour. Pour in the white wine, bring back to the boil, and add the stock. Reduce the heat, cover with a lid and simmer gently for about 2 hours or until the meat is very tender. To finish the ragü, stir in the cream and lemon juice and check for seasoning.

4. To make the parsnip purée, put the parsnips into a large pan of lightly salted cold water. Bring to the boil, then reduce the heat and simmer for 20–25 minutes or until tender.

5. Drain the parsnips well and if you want a truly smooth purée, push the cooked parsnips through a sieve using the back of a spatula (or, even better, use a mouli if you have one). Otherwise mash well using a potato masher.

6. Put the chocolate into a saucepan and bring the cream to a boil in another pan. Pour the cream over the chocolate and stir with a spatula until it has melted. Add the parsnip purée, mix well and season with salt and pepper. Reheat gently and serve with the rabbit sprinkled with parsley.

GÜ-LASH

We love the idea of dark unsweetened chocolate in a savoury dish. Not only does it enrich the sauce, but it also gives an extra depth of flavour. Goulash is a hearty and meaty (we've gone for beef) soup-come-stew which originates from Hungary and is just the dish to serve as a midweek meal with your family or friends. You could make it the night before as it reheats well. It is usually spiced up with paprika and chilli but we've gone one step further with the clever addition of chocolate from our chef Jerome.

SERVES 4–6

4 tbsp vegetable oil

3 onions, peeled and sliced

2 red peppers, cored, deseeded and sliced

2 carrots, peeled and sliced into rounds

5 garlic cloves, peeled and finely chopped

1.2kg stewing beef,
cut into bite-sized pieces

Pinch of curry powder

Pinch of chilli powder

4 green cardamom pods,
seeds removed and ground

3 tsp paprika

Salt and freshly ground black pepper

3 tbsp plain flour

4 tomatoes, roughly chopped

250ml red wine (about 2 glasses – Fred suggests a strong red wine like Merlot)

1–2 litres hot beef stock

80g dark chocolate (about 70% cocoa solids), broken into small pieces

500g packet of gnocchi, to serve

Small bunch of flat-leaf parsley, chopped, to serve

1. Heat 2 tablespoons of the oil in a large heavy-based pan or casserole. Add the onions, red peppers, carrots and garlic, and cook slowly for 15–20 minutes or until softened. Scoop out the vegetables with a slotted spoon and set aside.

2. Add one more tablespoon of oil to the pan, increase the heat and add half of the beef and fry until brown and caramelised all over. Don't be tempted to add it all in one hit (see the Gü tip below). Scrape the meat out into a bowl, add the remaining tablespoon of oil to the pan, then stir in the rest of the meat and caramelise as above.

3. Return the reserved meat to the pan, add all the spices and season with salt and pepper. Stir-fry for about a minute, then sprinkle with the flour and stir well.

4. Add the chopped tomatoes and then pour in the red wine, stir and let it bubble and thicken for a minute or two. Return the vegetables to the pan and pour over the beef stock to cover. Bring to the boil, cover, reduce the heat and let it simmer gently for 2–3 hours or until very tender. Check the pan occasionally to ensure the stew isn't drying out and add more stock if needed.

5. Just before serving, cook the gnocchi following the packet's instructions. Check the seasoning of the stew and stir in the chocolate until melted. Divide the gnocchi between 4–6 warmed bowls, ladle over the gü-lash and sprinkle with the parsley. Serve while it's piping hot and with the rest of the bottle of wine so that it doesn't go to waste.

GÜ TIP Frying too much meat in your pan at a time will cause it to boil rather than sauté and you won't achieve the caramelised brown meat you need to give the stew all its particular flavour and richness. So go easy, and put in small quantities at a time.

OPEN DARK CHOCOLATE VENISON RAVIOLE

WITH HERB SALAD

Chocolate and pasta? Different but deeply delicious ... if you are the proud owner of a pasta machine, then who are we to stop you from using it to make your own raviole for this dish? Use your favourite recipe and ensure that you roll the pasta through the machine several times, reducing the thickness setting each time. You might want to add some of the herbs from the salad to the dough. Finely chop a small handful of herbs and knead it into the mix before rolling out.

SERVES 4 AS A LIGHT LUNCH ... WITH SOME LEFT TO ENJOY THE NEXT DAY OR FREEZE FOR ANOTHER TIME

800g venison, cut into 5cm cubes

2 large onions, peeled

2 carrots, peeled

6 garlic cloves, peeled and crushed

Sprig of thyme

400ml red wine (Fred suggests a good strong red, like a Merlot)

3 tbsp vegetable oil

1 tbsp plain flour

Salt and freshly ground black pepper

400ml hot beef stock

8 sheets of fresh lasagne

50g dark chocolate (about 50% cocoa solids), chopped

Knob of unsalted butter, plus extra for brushing

FOR THE HERB SALAD

200g rocket, flat-leaf parsley and baby spinach leaves

Extra virgin olive oil

½ lemon

1. Tip the venison into a large bowl. Chop one of the onions and one of the carrots in half and put in a bowl with half the garlic and the sprig of thyme. Pour the red wine over the top and toss well to coat the meat. Cover and leave in the fridge overnight.

2. Next day, tip the marinated meat into a sieve set over a bowl to reserve the wine and pick out the vegetables, as they have now done their job.

3. In a large heavy-based pan or casserole, heat a tablespoon of the vegetable oil over a medium heat and brown the venison in two or three batches, adding a little more oil to the pan if needed. Brown well all over, scooping out each batch with a slotted spoon and keep warm. Meanwhile, chop the remaining onion and carrot.

4. Once all the meat has been browned, add the last spoon of oil, tip in the chopped vegetables and the remaining crushed garlic and cook for 5–6 minutes until softened and lightly browned.

5. Return the venison to the pan, sprinkle with the flour and stir well. Increase the heat and pour in the reserved wine, stirring to get any bits off the bottom of the pan. Bring to the boil and let it continue to boil until reduced by half. Season with salt and pepper.

6. Pour over the stock, give everything a good stir, cover and bring back up to the boil. Then reduce the heat and allow the pan or casserole's contents to simmer gently for 1–1½ hours or until tender. Towards the end, bring a large pan of lightly salted water to the boil for the pasta sheets.

recipe continues ...

7. Cut the lasagne sheets in half to make squares or rectangles. Drop the pasta into the boiling water and cook for 3–5 minutes until the pasta is just tender but still with a little bite.

8. Meanwhile, mix the salad leaves and herbs together in a serving bowl, drizzle with a little olive oil, add a squeeze of lemon juice and season with salt and pepper.

9. Drain the pasta well and, to finish the sauce, stir the chopped chocolate and knob of butter into the stew. To serve, place a square of pasta on each warmed dinner plate. Brush with a little melted butter. Spoon on some of the venison stew, cover with the remaining square of pasta, brush with a little more butter and top with the herb salad.

GÜ TIP Beef is a good option to replace the venison with for a slightly lighter meal and, for an extravagant slant, there is always wild boar.

GÜ TIP To make a more substantial dish, instead of the pasta, serve the stew with the polenta from Pan-fried Duck on Polenta with a Chocolate Orange Sauce (see page 185) or the White Chocolate and Parsnip Purée from the Rabbit Ragü or Vanilla Mash from Whole Chicken in a Cocoa Crust (see pages 151 and 212).

PORK MOLE

WITH BANANA AND AVOCADO CREAM

Mole (pronounced 'mol-ay') is a thick and spicy rich chocolate-tinged sauce served with meat that is very popular in Mexico. To further the taste sensation, we've added a smooth banana and avocado cream.

SERVES 4

2 tbsp olive oil

750g boned sliced pork belly

400g can of chopped tomatoes

400ml hot vegetable or chicken stock

200ml stout

90g dark chocolate (about 50% cocoa solids), chopped

1 tbsp smooth peanut butter

Salt and freshly ground black pepper

½ banana

1 ripe avocado, stoned and peeled

Juice of ½ a lime

Rice, to serve

Soured cream, to serve

FOR THE SPICE PASTE

1 yellow pepper, deseeded and chopped

½ tsp dried chipotle chilli

1 small scotch bonnet chilli, deseeded and chopped

1 green chilli, deseeded and chopped

1 red chilli, deseeded and chopped

1 onion, peeled and chopped

3 garlic cloves, peeled and chopped

30g ground almonds

40g raisins

1 tsp sesame seeds

2 tsp ground cumin

1 tsp ground cinnamon

½ tsp anise seed or fennel seed

1 tbsp light soft brown sugar

EQUIPMENT

Food processor

1. To make the spice paste, put all the ingredients in the bowl of a food processor, blitz to a smooth purée and set aside.

2. Heat the oil in a large heavy-based pan over a medium heat. Add the pork belly and cook until browned all over. Remove from the pan with a slotted spoon and set aside.

3. Add the chopped tomatoes to the pan and half of the stock. Bring to the boil, then reduce the heat, add the spice paste and stout and simmer, uncovered, for about 30 minutes to start reducing.

4. Add the chocolate and peanut butter and mix well. Then add the pork belly and stir in the remaining stock. Season with salt and pepper, cover and simmer gently for about 1½–2 hours until the meat is very tender, stirring occasionally to make sure it's not sticking. Check the seasoning.

5. Just before serving the mole, blend together the banana and avocado to a smooth consistency in the food processor with the lime juice. Divide the cooked rice between 4 warmed plates, top with the mole and serve with the banana, avocado and soured cream alongside.

. *for* SPECIAL DAYS AND HOLIDAYS

WHITE CHOCOLATE CHEESECAKE

WITH A SUMMER BERRY CHUTNEY

Although serving a chutney with a sweet dessert might sound unusual, the vanilla and fresh fruit meld together and the end result not only looks fantastic, but the flavour combinations are just gorgeous. To add some zing, you could include a little finely grated lime zest to the cheesecake mix.

SERVES 8

FOR THE CHEESECAKE

150g digestive biscuits

75g unsalted butter, melted

375g cream cheese

20g caster sugar

1 tbsp cornflour

1 egg yolk

180g white chocolate, broken into small pieces

100ml whipping cream

FOR THE SUMMER BERRY CHUTNEY

1 vanilla pod

1 cinnamon stick

100ml white wine vinegar

250g caster sugar

150g raspberries

150g blueberries

150g blackberries

EQUIPMENT

Food processor (optional)

20cm round springform cake tin

1. Preheat the oven to 130°C/Gas mark ½. Tip the biscuits into the food processor's bowl and blitz until they are finely crushed. Then, with the motor running, pour in the melted butter and mix just to combine. Alternatively, put the biscuits into a plastic bag and bash with a rolling pin. With a spoon, press the biscuit mixture evenly into the base of the tin.

2. Clean out the food processor bowl, if you've used one, and add the cream cheese, sugar, cornflour and egg yolk and blitz for 5 minutes until smooth, then scrape out into a bowl.

3. Put the chocolate pieces into a heatproof bowl. Pour the cream into a saucepan and bring it to the boil. Pour it over the chocolate and stir with a spatula until the chocolate has melted and become smooth.

4. Fold the warm chocolate ganache into the beaten cheese mixture and spoon it onto the biscuit base, making sure the surface is even.

5. Bake for 25–30 minutes or until the cheesecake is just starting to brown lightly around the edges, but it's still wobbly in the centre. Remove from the oven, leave to cool and then chill in the fridge for at least a couple of hours if not overnight.

6. To make the chutney, split the vanilla pod lengthways and scrape the tiny seeds that lay down its middle into a saucepan and drop in the pod. Add the cinnamon stick and pour in the vinegar and sugar. Bring to the boil, then reduce the heat and simmer until reduced by half, then stir in the berries.

7. Bring back to a simmer and remove from the heat. Leave to cool, then transfer to a bowl, cover and put in the fridge to chill. Remove the cinnamon stick and the vanilla pod when the chutney has cooled completely.

8. Run a hot knife around the edge of the cheesecake to help to unmould it, top with the berry chutney and serve cut into wedges.

EASTER EGGS

WITH A GÜ-EY SURPRISE CENTRE

Hidden inside a fluffy sweet white chocolate cream lies a bright orange, mango and passion fruit purée. Dip brioche soldiers deep into the shell for this Gü take on the real thing. We've used duck eggs as they are slightly larger, but you can use hen's eggs too. Get children to decorate and customise the eggshells, writing the names of the happy eaters on them.

MAKES 6

275ml whipping cream

1 tbsp liquid glucose or runny honey

Finely grated zest of 1 lime

100g white chocolate, broken into small pieces

12 duck or hen's eggs

1 mango

2 passion fruit

6 thick slices of brioche

EQUIPMENT

12 egg cups or shot glasses

Blender or small food processor

Electric hand mixer (optional)

1. Pour 75ml of the cream into a small saucepan, add the glucose or honey and bring to the boil. Remove from the heat, add the lime zest, cover with a lid and leave to infuse for 5 minutes.

2. Put the chocolate pieces into a large heatproof bowl. Then pour over the warm cream through a sieve and stir until the chocolate has melted and become smooth. Stir in the remaining cream and put in the fridge to chill completely.

3. To empty the duck eggs, with the flat side of a knife, give a gentle but firm tap on the pointed end of the egg. Then carefully pull away a neat circle of shell (or use an egg cutter, if you have one), big enough to be able to pour out the raw egg into a bowl (use the eggs later for a rich omelette or scrambled egg) and to get a teaspoon into the shell later on.

4. Rinse the eggs well with cold water, then stand them up in egg cups or shot glasses and pour boiling water into each one to sterilise. Tip out the water and leave to drain and dry upside down.

5. Meanwhile, peel the mango, cut away the flesh and drop it into a blender or small food processor and blitz until very smooth.

6. Cut the passion fruit in half and, with a spoon, scoop out the seeds and flesh into a sieve over a bowl. Pour the mango purée over the passion fruit and use the back of a spoon to push as much of the purée as possible through the sieve into the bowl.

7. When ready to serve, sit the shells, right-side up, in egg cups or shot glasses and use a teaspoon to divide the mango and passion fruit purée between them.

8. Whisk the white chocolate mixture to soft peaks by hand or with an electric hand mixer and spoon on top of the fruit purée.

9. Toast the brioche, cut into soldiers and serve warm with the eggs. Happy Easter!

CHOCOLATE FONDUE

WITH BANANA SPRING ROLLS & ROAST PINEAPPLE

As the ever-popular chocolate fondue only takes a few minutes to make, you will need to get your accompaniments and dippers ready in advance. Here we give you these recipes first for a choice of really pleasurable nibbles followed by the recipe for fondue itself to make the whole event one to savour.

SERVES 4

FOR THE BANANA SPRING ROLLS

25g unsalted butter

Two 46 x 24cm sheets of filo pastry

2 bananas

1 lime

25g dark chocolate (about 70% cocoa solids), finely grated

Icing sugar, for dusting

FOR THE ROAST PINEAPPLE

1 small ripe pineapple (about 700–750g total weight)

1 vanilla pod

100g caster sugar

100ml orange juice or 3 passion fruit, cut in half and seeds scraped out

FOR THE FONDUE

50g dark chocolate (about 70% cocoa solids), broken into small pieces

150g dark chocolate (about 50% cocoa solids), broken into small pieces

50g milk chocolate (34% minimum cocoa solids)

200ml whipping cream

1. To make either or both of the dippers, preheat the oven to 180°C/Gas mark 4. For the banana spring rolls, melt the butter in a small saucepan and use it to evenly brush the filo sheets, then cut each sheet into four. Cut the bananas in four lengthways and lay a piece of banana onto each rectangle of pastry. Finely grate lime zest over the top.

2. Sprinkle the grated chocolate over each piece of banana and roll them up in the pastry to form long cigars. Brush with butter again, place on a baking tray and bake for 15 minutes or until lightly golden. Dust with icing sugar to serve.

3. For the roast pineapple, cut off the crown of the pineapple with a sharp knife, and peel away the skin. Remove the eye spots by cutting long v-shaped shallow grooves along the outside of the fruit.

4. Cut the vanilla pod into four. Using a small sharp knife or a chopstick, bore four random little holes into the pineapple and push the vanilla pieces inside each one.

5. Tip the sugar into a saucepan and add 1 tablespoon of water. Heat gently for 3–4 minutes without stirring until the sugar has dissolved and turned a golden brown colour. Add the pineapple to the caramel and turn to coat, then add the orange juice or cut passion fruit seeds.

6. Carefully transfer the pineapple and any juices to a small baking dish and bake for about 45 minutes, basting with the juices, every so often. Serve it at the table and carve in to chunks to dip into the fondue.

7. To make the fondue, put all the chocolate pieces into a heatproof bowl. Pour the cream into a small saucepan and bring it to the boil. Pour it over the chocolate and stir with a spatula until the chocolate has melted and become smooth. Serve straight away with either or both of our dipper recipes above and the additional ideas described overleaf.

recipe continues ...

OTHER GÜ DIPPING SUGGESTIONS Caramelised Popcorn or Puffed Rice (see page 34), Macadamia Nut Brownies or White Chocolate Blondies (see pages 72 and 68), Cherries soaked in Kirsch (aka griottines), Sesame Nougatine (see page 32), Chocolate Grissini, minus the chocolate coating (see page 53), Candied Citrus Fruit (see page 36) and Viennese Biscuits (see page 96).

CHOCOLATE SALTED CARAMEL & PEANUT TART

You can never have enough options on a chocolate tart and this twist on the classic also makes use of our Chocolate Sweetcrust Pastry case (see page 29).

SERVES 10–12

1 x 26cm round Chocolate Sweetcrust Pastry case (see page 29)

FOR THE SALTED CARAMEL AND PEANUT FILLING

1 quantity homemade or shop-bought Gü Chocolate Ganache (see page 30)

1 tbsp liquid glucose or runny honey

100g caster sugar

150ml double cream

Pinch of sea salt

150g crunchy or smooth peanut butter

1. Make the Chocolate Sweetcrust Pastry case and set aside. Then make (or buy) the Gü Chocolate Ganache and keep it at room temperature.

2. To make the salted caramel sauce, warm the glucose or honey in a high-sided pan and stir in the sugar with 1 teaspoon of water. Heat gently for 3–4 minutes without stirring until the sugar has dissolved and turned a golden brown colour.

3. Warm the cream in another saucepan and set aside. Remove the pan of caramel from the heat and, protecting your hands as it may splutter, gradually and very carefully stir one third of the warm cream into the caramel. Mix together and then stir in the remaining cream.

4. Bring the sauce back to the boil then remove the pan from the heat. Stir in the salt, let the sauce cool down and then put in the fridge to chill.

5. Spread the peanut butter evenly over the base and then spread with the salted caramel sauce. Finally, pour the ganache all over to cover and leave the tart in the fridge for a few hours to set.

his son. Although it can get messy making these with kids, the fun comes from seeing them having a great time with food. We've given you a choice of yummy fillings and coatings: if you're feeling extra showy-offy or have a party in mind, you could make both. Double the meringue quantities then fill and decorate half of them with dark chocolate and the rest with white.

MAKES 8

3 egg whites

90g caster sugar

90g icing sugar

FOR THE DARK CHOCOLATE MERINGUES

300g homemade or shop-bought Gü Chocolate Ganache (see page 30)

200g dark chocolate (about 50 or 70% cocoa solids), melted (see page 10)

50g grated dark chocolate (about 50 or 70% cocoa solids) or 25g chopped nuts

FOR THE WHITE CHOCOLATE AND COCONUT MERINGUES

100ml coconut milk

150g white chocolate, broken into small pieces and 200g melted (see page 10)

25g desiccated coconut, plus 2 tbsp to decorate

1 tbsp Malibu liqueur

EQUIPMENT

Electric hand mixer

Piping bag fitted with a 1cm straight nozzle

1. Preheat the oven to 110°C/Gas mark ¼ and line a couple of baking trays with baking parchment.

2. To make the meringue, whisk the egg whites with an electric hand mixer in a bowl to soft peaks, then gradually whisk in the sugar until the mixture resembles shaving foam. Using a metal spoon, carefully fold in the icing sugar.

3. Pipe the meringue into 16 domes on the prepared trays and bake for about 45 minutes, keeping an eye on them. The meringue should be firm and still have a nice white colour; too yellow and they will have been overbaked or the oven was too hot. To check that they are sufficiently well cooked, take one of the meringues out of the oven, let it cool for a couple of minutes and then tap the bottom of it to see if it is dry enough. If it sounds hollow, remove the rest from the oven and leave them to cool completely on a wire rack.

4. For the dark chocolate meringues, make (or buy) the ganache and spread a little dollop of it on the flat side of a meringue, sandwich with another and return the fully formed meringue to the baking parchment. Repeat with the remaining mixture. Brush the melted chocolate all over the meringues and sprinkle with the grated chocolate or nuts.

5. For the white chocolate and coconut meringues, first make the filling. Pour the coconut milk into a small saucepan and bring to the boil. Remove the pan from the heat, drop in the 150g of chocolate pieces and stir until it has melted and become smooth. Stir in the 25g of desiccated coconut and the liqueur, then pour the mixture into a bowl and leave to cool. Chill in the fridge for 4–6 hours until set.

recipe continues ...

6. Spread a little dollop of the white chocolate and coconut ganache on the flat side of a meringue, sandwich with another and return the fully formed meringue to the baking parchment. Repeat with the remaining mixture. Brush over the melted white chocolate and sprinkle with the desiccated coconut.

GÜ TIP By toasting the coconut you bring out its nutty flavour still further. Preheat the oven to 180°C/Gas mark 4 and tip the desiccated coconut for the topping onto a baking tray. Toast for a couple of minutes, stirring occasionally, until lightly golden. Keep a close eye on the coconut; it can burn all too easily. Tip onto a plate to cool and then sprinkle over the meringues.

EASY CHOCOLATE MOUSSE CAKE

Love chocolate mousse and chocolate cake? Why choose? This elegant and silky smooth mousse cake is easiest to make in a springform cake tin. When it comes to sandwiching the cake with our chocolate mousse and then adding more mousse on the top it's by far and away simpler to do it in the tin. Once it is set, all you then have to do is unclip the tin surround and slide the cake onto your favourite serving plate.

SERVES 12–16

FOR THE CHOCOLATE SPONGE

150g plain flour

3 tsp baking powder

300g dark chocolate (about 70% cocoa solids), broken into small pieces, plus extra for chocolate curls to decorate (see page 12)

200g unsalted butter

6 eggs

300g granulated sugar

FOR THE CHOCOLATE MOUSSE

200g dark chocolate (about 50% cocoa solids), broken into pieces

225ml whipping cream

FOR THE RICH CHOCOLATE GLAZE (OPTIONAL)

5g gelatine leaf (about 3 leaves)

75g dark chocolate (about 70% cocoa solids), broken into small pieces

75g caster sugar

75ml liquid glucose

50g condensed milk

EQUIPMENT

20cm round springform cake tin

Stick blender

1. Preheat the oven to 170°C/Gas mark 3 and line the cake tin with baking parchment. Sift the flour and baking powder together into a bowl.

2. Put the chocolate and butter into a small saucepan over a low heat and stir well until melted and smooth.

3. Lightly beat the eggs and the sugar together in a bowl until only just combined. Stir in the chocolate mixture and then fold in the flour and baking powder.

4. Scrape the mixture into the prepared tin and bake for 45–50 minutes or until when a skewer is inserted in the centre it comes out clean. Leave to cool in the tin for 5 minutes, then turn out onto a wire rack and leave to cool completely.

5. Line the springform tin again with baking parchment, cut the sponge in half across its middle and place one half in the base of the tin.

6. To make the mousse, put the chocolate and 75ml of the cream in a heatproof bowl over a pan of gently simmering water. Stir occasionally until the chocolate has melted and the mixture is smooth. Leave to cool very slightly for 5 minutes. Whip the remaining cream until it forms soft peaks and fold into the chocolate mixture. Pour half of the mousse onto the cake in the tin, cover with the second half of the cake and pour over the remaining mousse, levelling the surface. Place in the fridge for a couple of hours to set.

7. If you are also making the rich chocolate glaze read the tip on page 170, then soak the gelatine in 2 tablespoons of water in a bowl and put the chocolate in a heatproof bowl. At the same time, put the sugar and liquid glucose in a saucepan with 50ml of water and bring to the boil. Pour the hot syrup over the chocolate and stir with a spatula until the chocolate is melted and smooth.

recipe continues ...

8. Squeeze the gelatine and add to the hot chocolate together with the condensed milk. Stir until the gelatine has melted and then make extra smooth with a stick blender, being careful not to incorporate any air bubbles. Leave the glaze to cool, overnight if possible, and then reheat to room temperature.

9. Remove the cake from the fridge. Unmould it from the tin and slide the cake directly onto a pretty serving plate, leaving the baking parchment behind. (If you are making the glaze, slide it onto a wire rack.) Artistically decorate your creation with chocolate curls or shards of Chocolate Bubble Wrap (see pages 12 and 194).

GÜ TIP We've given you a recipe for a rich chocolate glaze for extra special occasions (see steps 7 and 8 above for instructions). If you are using this glaze, for best results prepare it the day before. Make a third of the sponge quantity in this recipe to use as the base (reduce the baking time slightly) and double the quantity suggested for the mousse. Assemble the single layer of cake with one thick layer of mousse on top, so that the glaze will stick and set directly onto the mousse. Remove the cake from the fridge, unmould it from the tin onto a wire rack. Then pour the glaze all over the cake, ensuring it flows down the sides to completely coat them. Tap the wire rack to remove the excess glaze and place on your serving plate. Decorate as you fancy!

CHOCOLATE, CARDAMOM & CLEMENTINE MARBLED ROULADE

A roulade always looks spectacular, especially for a Christmas celebration, so don't be put off by the thought of rolling the meringue base around the gü-ey citrus cream filling. Simply use some parchment paper lightly dusted with caster sugar to help you. It will prevent your fingers from getting sticky.

SERVES 4–6

FOR THE MERINGUE

75g dark chocolate
(about 70% cocoa solids)

4 egg whites

6 green cardamom pods, seeds removed and ground

Pinch of salt

200g golden caster sugar, plus 4 tbsp

300ml whipping cream

Finely grated zest and juice
of 1 clementine

TO DECORATE

Icing sugar

Cocoa powder

Edible gold dust

EQUIPMENT

23 x 30cm Swiss roll tin

Electric hand mixer

1. Preheat the oven to 180°C/Gas mark 4. Line the Swiss roll tin with baking parchment.

2. Break 50g of the chocolate into a heatproof bowl and melt (see page 10). Whisk the egg whites, ground cardamom and salt together with an electric hand mixer in a bowl to soft peaks, then gradually whisk in the 200g of caster sugar until the mixture resembles shaving foam.

3. Drizzle some of the melted chocolate backwards and forwards over the meringue in the bowl and scoop out spoonfuls, placing them evenly over the lined tin. Add more chocolate to the bowl each time you take out a spoonful of meringue.

4. Carefully spread the meringue out evenly and drizzle any remaining chocolate over the surface. Bake for about 15 minutes until crisp on the outside. Remove from the oven and leave to cool completely.

5. Lay a piece of fresh baking parchment on a work surface. Sprinkle with 2 tablespoons of caster sugar and flip the meringue over onto it. Carefully pull away the used paper.

6. Finely chop the remaining chocolate. Whip together the cream with most of the clementine zest (reserving the rest for decoration) and juice and the remaining 2 tablespoons of caster sugar in a large bowl until it forms soft peaks. Then stir in the chopped chocolate.

7. Spread the cream over the roulade and roll the meringue up lengthways using the paper to help turn it over. Place on a serving dish and dust lightly with icing sugar, cocoa, the reserved clementine zest and edible gold dust. A pud fit for a king.

GÜ TIP Sprinkle ground pistachios or pomegranate seeds over the roulade for an even more textured taste sensation.

SPIRAL CHOCOLATE LOLLIPOPS

We think that you're never too old to enjoy a lollipop, especially ones like this made with white, dark and milk chocolate. There is also the golden opportunity to enjoy many a different coating – just choose from our suggestions below. The lollies are also especially good fun to make with children.

MAKES ABOUT 12

50g white chocolate, broken into small pieces

100g dark chocolate (about 50 or 70% cocoa solids), broken into small pieces

50g milk chocolate (34% minimum cocoa solids), broken into small pieces

FOR THE COATING, CHOOSE FROM:

Crushed amaretti

Popping candy

Crumbled honeycomb

Chopped pistachios, hazelnuts, pecans, peanuts or nuts of your choice

Chopped dried fruits

Extra melted chocolate in contrasting colour

EQUIPMENT

Piping bag or a teaspoon

12 lollipop sticks or wooden skewers

1. Line a couple of baking trays with baking parchment. Melt the chocolate(s) of your choice in separate bowls (see page 10) and spoon the chocolate into the piping bag, if using. Snip a tiny piece off the end of the piping bag and pipe the chocolate onto the prepared baking trays to make spiral discs of choccie. Alternatively, you might find it easier to simply put a dessertspoonful (or more) of the melted chocolate onto the parchment and allow it to spread into its natural shape.

2. Alternatively, for mixed chocolate lollies, use a teaspoon to drizzle the chocolate in circles, then repeat with the other two chocolates.

3. Push a lollipop stick or wooden skewer into the middle of each lollipop, and sprinkle or drizzle over your choice of coating. Pop in the fridge until they've set and then tuck in.

GÜ TIP To make the feathered pattern that we've used on one of the lollipops in the photograph, drizzle or pipe lines of melted (in this case, white) chocolate over the lollipop. Then drag the tip of a cocktail stick across the lines and – simple! – they are joined together. For a more cobweb-like effect, alternate the direction in which you drag the cocktail stick.

CHOCOLATE SPONGE BIRTHDAY CAKE

A chocolate sponge cake has to be the highlight of a birthday celebration. Here we've created a double layer of light and moist chocolate sponge that is not only topped with a chocolate glaze, but filled with it too. Don't worry if the sponge sinks slightly on cooling – the icing will quickly cover that up.

SERVES 12–16

FOR THE CHOCOLATE SPONGE

150g plain flour

4 tsp baking powder

300g dark chocolate (about 70% cocoa solids), broken into small pieces

200g unsalted butter

6 eggs

300g granulated sugar

FOR THE CHOCOLATE FILLING AND GLAZE

500g dark chocolate (about 50% cocoa solids), broken into small pieces

400ml whipping cream

2 tbsp liquid glucose or runny honey

100g unsalted butter, cut into pieces

EQUIPMENT

2 x 20cm round cake tins

Stick blender

1. Preheat the oven to 170°C/Gas mark 3 and line the cake tins with baking parchment. Sift the flour and baking powder together into a bowl.

2. Put the chocolate and butter into a small saucepan over a low heat and stir well until they have melted and become smooth. Alternatively, melt them in a microwave on low power, checking and stirring regularly (see page 10).

3. Lightly beat the eggs and the sugar together in a bowl until only just combined. Stir in the chocolate mixture and then fold in the flour and baking powder.

4. Divide the mixture equally between the lined tins and bake for 30–40 minutes or until when a skewer inserted in the centre comes out clean. Leave to cool in the tins for 5 minutes, then turn out onto a wire rack and leave to cool completely.

5. For the chocolate filling and glaze, tip the chocolate into a heatproof bowl. Pour the cream into a small saucepan, add the glucose or honey and bring to the boil. Pour the mixture over the chocolate and stir with a spatula until it has melted and become smooth. Now add the butter and stir until fully incorporated and then finish with a quick whizz on the hand blender.

6. Pour half of the mixture into a bowl and leave to cool and almost set. Leave the remaining chocolate mixture in the pan and set aside.

7. Place one piece of sponge on a wire rack set over a tray. Spread the sponge with the almost-set chocolate filling and cover with the remaining layer of cake.

8. Place the remaining chocolate mixture back on a low heat and melt gently. Pour the glaze evenly over the cake on the rack, letting it drip down the sides (or spread it around the sides with a palette knife), to cover completely. Add the necessary number of birthday candles, light, carry through to the birthday boy or girl, sing Happy Birthday and then enjoy your creation.

CHOCOLATE & PEACH KNICKERBOCKER GLORY

Always a childhood delight, but why stop the fun when you grow up? The wonders of a knickerbocker glory will never fail to please. For the very best results, serve the chocolate sauce slightly warmed.

MAKES 6

3 ripe peaches

150g raspberries

50g light soft brown sugar

3 tbsp amaretto liqueur

50g white chocolate, chopped

300ml whipping cream

2 tsp caster sugar

6 amaretti halves

Vanilla ice cream, enough for 2 scoops per person

25g toasted blanched almonds, finely chopped

FOR THE CHOCOLATE SAUCE

25g unsalted butter

125ml double cream

2 tbsp golden syrup or runny honey

100g dark chocolate (about 50% cocoa solids), broken into small pieces

EQUIPMENT

6 tall glasses

1. Preheat the oven to 180°C/Gas mark 4. Cut the peaches in half and remove their stones, cut into wedges and tip into a small baking dish with half of the raspberries.

2. Sprinkle the peaches and raspberries evenly with the brown sugar and amaretto, toss well, cover with foil and bake for 30–35 minutes or until tender. Remove from the oven, stir in the white chocolate and set aside.

3. To make the chocolate sauce, place the butter, double cream, syrup or honey and dark chocolate in a saucepan over a low heat for 4–5 minutes, stirring occasionally, until the sauce has melted and become smooth. Set aside.

4. Whip the whipping cream and caster sugar together in a large bowl until it forms soft peaks.

5. Crumble the amaretti into the base of the glasses and spoon over the cooked peaches and raspberries. Add a scoop or two of vanilla ice cream, scatter with the remaining raspberries, and pipe or spoon over the sweetened cream. Then drizzle with the chocolate sauce and sprinkle with the nuts. Serve with long spoons and a smile.

GÜ TIP As if there wasn't enough excitement in these glasses already, consider adding some shards of Sesame Nougatine (see page 32) for further decoration or in place of the nuts.

PROFITEROLES

WITH ALMOND CHANTILLY CREAM

These are a mighty fine treat. While we've suggested that the craquelin part of the recipe is optional, it does give the top of the profiteroles a wonderful crunchy topping, so if you have the time and energy, it's definitely worth giving it a try.

MAKES ABOUT 30 PROFITEROLES

1 quantity Choux Pastry with a Crispy Craquelin Topping (see page 22)

1 quantity homemade Gü Chocolate Ganache (see page 30)

FOR THE ALMOND CHANTILLY CREAM

75g marzipan, chopped into pieces

375ml whipping cream

25g caster sugar

EQUIPMENT

Electric hand mixer

Piping bag fitted with a 1cm piping nozzle

1. Make the profiteroles with their crispy craquelin topping.

2. To make the almond Chantilly cream, put the marzipan in a heatproof bowl. Pour 50ml of the whipping cream into a saucepan and bring it to the boil. Pour it over the marzipan, add the sugar and whisk together until the marzipan has fully dissolved and become smooth. Leave to cool completely in the fridge for at least 2 hours.

3. Add the remaining whipping cream to the sugar and marzipan mixture and whip with an electric hand mixer until they form soft peaks. Fill the piping bag with the Chantilly cream.

4. Cut the profiteroles in half across their middles and pipe Chantilly cream onto the base, top with the top half of the choux bun and sit on a wire rack set over a tray.

5. Now make the ganache so that it is warm. Carefully pour a spoonful of the ganache over each profiterole and pop it back on the wire rack. Leave them to set. If you need to speed up the setting process, put the rack in the fridge.

MONKFISH

WITH A CHOCOLATE & SHALLOT SAUCE & FENNEL SALAD

As pieces of fish go, monkfish is relatively dense and fleshy so can withstand a robust chocolate and shallot sauce, which is exactly why we've suggested this combination. If you can't get hold of monkfish (or fancy a change), then line-caught cod is a fine substitute.

SERVES 4

3 tbsp olive oil

1 large shallot, peeled and very finely chopped

Sprig of thyme

150ml white wine

Salt and freshly ground black pepper

25g dark chocolate (about 50% cocoa solids), broken into small pieces

250ml whipping cream

1 lemon, cut in half

Knob of unsalted butter

1 large monkfish tail, boned and skinned (700g of fillets total weight)

1 large bulb of fennel

1. Heat 1 tablespoon of the oil in a saucepan over a low heat, add the shallot and thyme and cook for 5–6 minutes or until the shallots are tender and lightly golden.

2. Increase the heat, pour in the white wine and let it simmer to reduce by half or until the liquid is slightly syrupy. Season with salt and pepper and then remove the pan from the heat. Stir in the chocolate until it has melted and become smooth.

3. Place the pan back on a medium heat and stir in the cream. Simmer to reduce by one third, add a squeeze of lemon juice (about a teaspoon), and adjust the seasoning once more. Set aside and keep warm.

4. Preheat the oven to 180°C/Gas mark 4. Heat the remaining oil and the butter in an ovenproof frying pan or heavy roasting tin on the hob over a medium heat. Add the monkfish fillets and cook them until they are lightly browned all over, turning every 30 seconds or so.

5. Transfer the pan or roasting tin to the oven and cook for 3 minutes, then remove and set aside to rest for 5 minutes. While the fish is resting, make the fennel salad. Snip off any green feathery fronds from the fennel top, chop them up and set aside. Trim the bottom off the bulb and cut it in half lengthways. Cut out the core, then slice the fennel into wafer-thin pieces with a mandolin or swivel peeler.

6. Put the slices in a bowl, sprinkle with salt and pepper, add a squeeze of lemon juice and the fennel fronds, and toss well.

7. To serve, slice the monkfish and arrange on warmed dinner plates. Spoon over some of the sauce and serve with the fennel salad alongside.

CHOCOLATE BLINIS

WITH SMOKED SALMON & POACHED LEMON

These mouth-watering morsels make perfect canapés to serve at a party or for pre-meal nibbles. They are a classic combination, but with the twist of cocoa powder stirred into the blini mix they look stunning too.

MAKES ABOUT 20

2 lemons

50g caster sugar, plus 1 tbsp

2 eggs

50g plain flour

½ tsp baking powder

1 tbsp cocoa powder

5 tbsp milk

Pinch of salt

2–3 tbsp vegetable oil

TO SERVE

200ml crème fraîche

200g smoked salmon

1 cooked beetroot (not in vinegar), cut into 1.5cm cubes

Handful of pea shoots or sprigs of dill, leaves removed

EQUIPMENT

Electric hand mixer

1. First make the poached lemon. Using a sharp knife, peel the skin and pith off the lemons. Then, cutting on either side of the membrane, remove the segments one by one.

2. Tip the 50g of sugar into a small saucepan with 100ml of water and bring to the boil. Remove the pan from the heat and slide the lemon segments into the syrup. Leave to cool at room temperature.

3. When ready to serve, separate the eggs, putting the whites into one bowl and the yolks into another (scrupulously clean) one. Sift the flour, baking powder and cocoa powder together into a further bowl.

4. Add the milk to the egg yolks and mix with the dry ingredients to make a smooth thick batter. Add the salt and the tablespoon of sugar to the egg whites and whisk with an electric hand mixer until until they form stiff peaks. With a metal spoon, mix one third of the whisked egg whites into the batter, then gently fold in the rest.

5. Heat a non-stick pan on a medium heat, add a little of the oil, then pour small spoonfuls of the batter into the hot pan and fry for 20–30 seconds on each side. Remove them with a fish slice and keep them warm while continuing to make blinis with the rest of the batter.

6. To serve, spoon a little crème fraîche on top of each blini, top with smoked salmon, a couple cubes of beetroot, a segment of poached lemon and a couple of pea shoot or dill leaves.

PAN-FRIED DUCK ON POLENTA

WITH A CHOCOLATE ORANGE SAUCE

No book containing chocolate recipes would be complete without a chocolate sauce to accompany a good piece of meat. So here it is! A chocolate and orange sauce made with chicken stock to pour around a quickly seared duck breast.

SERVES 4

500ml milk

75g quick-cook polenta

Salt and freshly ground black pepper

4 duck breasts (about 200g each)

1 radicchio or 2 baby gem lettuce, cut in half lengthways, or wide strips of Swiss chard leaves

1 tbsp olive oil

FOR THE SAUCE

1½ tbsp caster sugar

3 tbsp red wine vinegar

200ml orange juice

400ml hot chicken stock

50g dark chocolate (about 50% cocoa solids), chopped

Finely grated zest of ¼ orange

25g unsalted butter

1. To make the sauce, first tip the sugar into a deep saucepan and add 1 tablespoon of water. Heat gently for 3–4 minutes without stirring until the sugar has dissolved and turned a golden brown colour. Carefully (because it will splutter), pour in the red wine vinegar, let it bubble and then reduce by half. Add the orange juice and stock and let it reduce again, this time by more than half, and set aside.

2. Pour the milk into a large saucepan and bring to the boil. Add the polenta in a steady stream, whisking continuously until it thickens and then continue stirring for a further minute. Remove the pan from the heat, season with salt and pepper, cover and set aside.

3. Season the duck breasts on both sides, then sear, skin-side down in a large frying pan or griddle pan over a high heat. Cook for 8–9 minutes on each side (slightly less if you want the duck rarer, or slightly more if you like it more well cooked). Set aside in a warm place for 10 minutes to rest.

4. Drizzle the radicchio, baby gem or Swiss chard with the oil, season and place on a griddle pan or frying pan. Cook for only about 30 seconds on each side or until just wilted.

5. Return the pan of sauce to the heat and bring it back to the boil. Finish the sauce by whisking in the chocolate, orange zest and the butter and season.

6. Divde the polenta between 4 warmed soup plates and add the wilted leaves. Slice each duck breast and place on top, then spoon over some chocolate sauce and serve immediately.

GÜ TIP Go to a good butcher and buy pigeon or guinea fowl breasts as an alternative to the duck. Some steamed green beans instead of the raddichio also work well, as does good old mashed potato in place of the polenta.

SCALLOPS
WITH A SESAME CRUST & CHOCOLATE DRESSING

This recipe makes an ideal starter. The light sesame crust and dressing spruced up with a hint of chocolate only serve to enhance the sweet juicy scallops resting on their bed of leeks.

SERVES 4

50g unsalted butter

1 large leek, thinly sliced, washed thoroughly and drained

Salt and freshly ground black pepper

16 scallops, trimmed and roe removed

4 tbsp sesame seeds

2 tbsp olive oil

FOR THE CHOCOLATE DRESSING

2 tbsp rice vinegar

2 tbsp sake

4 tbsp soy sauce

25g dark chocolate (about 50% cocoa solids), chopped

1. Melt the butter in a large frying pan over a low heat, add the leek, season it with salt and pepper, then cover with a lid and cook gently for 5 minutes or until softened.

2. Rinse the scallops thoroughly, then pat dry on kitchen paper and season on both sides. Tip the sesame seeds onto a plate and press the flat side of each scallop into them.

3. For the chocolate dressing, pour the vinegar, sake and soy sauce into a small saucepan and heat to a simmer. Remove the pan from the heat, add the chocolate and stir until it has melted and become smooth.

4. Heat the oil in a large frying pan over a medium heat and add the scallops, flat-side down. Fry them for about 30 seconds on each side, depending on their size, or until just tender and lightly golden. Serve immediately on a bed of the warm leeks with a drizzle of the chocolate dressing and the rest alongside.

GÜ TIP Don't be tempted to overcrowd the pan or the temperature will drop and the scallops will boil rather than caramelise, so do this in batches or two pans if necessary.

... for **CHOCOLATE EXTREMISTS**

COCONUT SNOWBALL PROFITEROLES

WITH COCONUT SNOW

This is the treat of all treats – mouthfuls of pure indulgence. They may need a bit of time to make, but oh so impressive for a dinner party. Your plan of action is to first make the coconut snow, then bake the profiteroles (with or without the craquelin topping), make the Gü chocolate ganache (if you haven't grabbed some in the supermarket already) and finally whip up the Chantilly cream just before you finally serve. Phew!

SERVES 10

400ml can of coconut milk

50g caster sugar

1 quantity Choux Pastry Buns
(see page 22)

1 homemade or shop-bought quantity
Gü Chocolate Ganache (see page 30)

2 quantities Chantilly Cream
(see page 20)

Mango sorbet, enough for 3 small scoops
per person

25g desiccated coconut

EQUIPMENT

Food processor

1. For the coconut snow, pour the coconut milk into a plastic container, stir in the caster sugar and freeze overnight until solid.

2. Make the profiteroles followed by the ganache.

3. When ready to serve, take the frozen coconut milk from the freezer and run warm water on its base to loosen. Tip the frozen coconut milk onto a clean tea towel and bash into chunks with a rolling pin. Tip them into a food processor and blitz to create snow. Magic! Return the snow to its container and then put it back into the freezer.

4. Make the Chantilly cream and warm your ganache and now you are poised, ready for action to create these mouth-watering morsels:
   - Cut the profiteroles in half.
   - Place the base of three profiteroles on each plate.
   - Spoon a small scoop of sorbet onto each one.
   - Cover with the top half of each profiterole and press gently.
   - Use the back of a spoon to spread some Chantilly cream over the top of each choux bun.
   - Sprinkle with desiccated coconut.

5. Serve at the table, pouring some warm chocolate ganache around the profiteroles and adding a spoonful of the coconut snow on the side of each plate.

GÜ TIP If you can't find mango sorbet, coconut is just as successful in this dish.

TEMPERING CHOCOLATE

If you want your chocolate to have a high-gloss finish, then tempering is the way forward. It involves melting chocolate by raising and lowering its temperature to even out the crystals of cocoa butter, giving a shiny, crisp result. It sounds tricky and there are a variety of methods out there, but we use 'seeding' - unmelted chocolate is added to melted, changing the temperature. We're using 500g chocolate, which is the minimum quantity to work with in order to control the temperature process.

500g dark chocolate of your choice, chopped

EQUIPMENT

Heatproof bowl and pan

Sugar thermometer that shows as low as 26°C

TO TEMPER ON A HOB

1. Put 200g of the chocolate into a heatproof bowl and set over a saucepan of barely simmering water. Stir until is has melted and then heat until the chocolate temperature reaches 40–45°C.

2. Remove the bowl from the saucepan and stir in the remaining chocolate (ensure the water in the pan remains simmering). Mix the two chocolates together, stirring constantly, to lower the temperature to 28–29°C.

3. Put the bowl back on the pan and reheat the chocolate, stirring occasionally, until it goes back up to 31–32°C for dark chocolate. The chocolate is now crystallised and ready to use.

TO TEMPER USING A MICROWAVE

1. For an 800W microwave, tip the 200g of chocolate into a microwaveproof bowl and place in the oven on medium power. Melt the chocolate for 30 seconds.

2. Stir the chocolate, heat again for 15 seconds and, if not fully melted, heat for a further 15 seconds. (Be very careful not to overcook as this will burn the chocolate.) Check the temperature of your chocolate as it needs to be 40–45°C.

3. Continuously stir in the remaining chocolate until the temperature lowers to 28–29°C. Heat the chocolate again in 15-second bursts, or until the chocolate reaches 31–32°C for dark chocolate. The chocolate is now crystallised and ready to use.

GÜ TIP The temperatures for milk and white chocolate are:
Milk chocolate: lower to 27–28°C, then increase to 29–30°C
White chocolate: lower to 26–27C, then increase to 28–29°C.

CHOCOLATE BUBBLE WRAP

This simple yet creative idea will wow your guests. Snap it into shards to pop on the top of the Pot au Chocolat or Raspberry Chocolate Mousse Pots (see pages 123 and 110), simply serve with coffee at elevenses, tea time or after an evening meal – or even all three!

MAKES LOTS OF CHOCOLATE BUBBLE WRAP

200g dark chocolate (about 50 or 70% cocoa solids), melted

EQUIPMENT

Two 22 x 20cm pieces of washed bubble wrap

1. Temper the chocolate, as described on page 193. Lay each piece of the bubble wrap on a baking tray, then pour the melted chocolate over the bubble wrap and spread it evenly to create a thin layer.

2. Put the trays in the fridge to chill. When the chocolate has hardened, peel it from the bubble wrap and enjoy.

CHOCOLATE MILLEFEUILLE

WITH CHOCOLATE CHANTILLY CREAM

Millefeuille means 'thousand leaves' in French and in this dessert it refers to the many delicate layers created by folding the pastry numerous times during the making of puff pastry. When cooked, this creates lots of crisp delicate layers that melt in the mouth. This extra-special millefeuille also has a caramelised pastry top with a thick chocolate Chantilly cream in between.

SERVES 6–8

500g ready-made puff pastry

Icing sugar, for dusting

50g dark chocolate, grated

FOR THE CHOCOLATE CHANTILLY CREAM

200g milk chocolate (34% minimum cocoa solids), broken into small pieces

400ml whipping cream

3 tsp honey

EQUIPMENT

Electric hand mixer (optional)

Piping bag fitted with a 1cm piping nozzle (optional)

1. To make the chocolate Chantilly cream, put the chocolate pieces into a heatproof bowl. Pour 100ml of the cream into a saucepan, add the honey and bring to the boil. Pour it over the chocolate and stir with a spatula until the chocolate has melted and become smooth. Then stir in the remaining cream, cover and leave to cool. Chill in the fridge for 3–4 hours or overnight.

2. Line a baking tray with baking parchment. Roll the puff pastry into a rectangle measuring about 45 x 30cm and place it on the baking tray, cover with cling film and place in the fridge for 30 minutes.

3. Preheat the oven to 180°C/Gas mark 4. Place the tray of pastry in the oven and bake for 25–30 minutes or until crisp, risen and golden. Remove the tray from the oven and increase the oven temperature to 240°C/Gas mark 9.

4. Place another tray on top of the pastry and press gently to even the layers. Remove the top tray and, using a fine sieve, dust a thin layer of icing sugar all over the surface of the pastry. Return the tray to the oven for 5–8 minutes, turning the tray every so often, to caramelise the tops to a golden brown.

5. Remove the tray from the oven once again and, while the puff pastry is still warm, cut it into three 15 x 30cm rectangles using a serrated knife. Trim the edges to neaten and leave the pastry to cool on a wire rack.

6. Whip the chocolate Chantilly cream until it forms soft peaks. Spoon some of the mixture into the piping bag fitted with the nozzle (be careful not to overfill as it will be tricky to use) and pipe out 1cm blobs of cream in neat rows across two of the pastry rectangles. Top up the bag as necessary. (Alternatively, avoid piping and simply spread the Chantilly cream evenly over two of the pastry rectangles.) Then grate a little chocolate over the top. Place one of these topped pastries on a serving plate and top with another (but don't be tempted to press down). Finish with the remaining pastry and decorate with a dusting of icing sugar.

PIÑA COLADA MACAROONS

We've turned this classic eighties' cocktail, which combines the Caribbean flavours of pineapple, coconut and rum, into delicious soft macaroons with a creamy white chocolate ganache filling.

MAKES ABOUT 25

125g ground almonds

125g icing sugar

3 egg whites, lightly beaten

125g caster sugar, plus 2 tsp

Pinch of salt

FOR THE GANACHE

50g peeled, cored and chopped pineapple

225g white chocolate

2 tbsp coconut milk

1 tsp lime juice

1 tbsp honey

25g unsalted butter, diced

2 tsp white rum

TO DECORATE

150g white chocolate, for coating

50g desiccated coconut

EQUIPMENT

Food processor

Electric hand mixer

Sugar thermometer (optional)

Piping bag fitted with a 1cm piping nozzle

1. First make the ganache filling. Put the pineapple in a food processor and blitz to a purée. Put the chocolate pieces into a heatproof bowl. Pour the coconut milk, lime juice and honey into a small saucepan, stir in the pineapple purée and bring to the boil. Pour the mixture over the chocolate and stir with a spatula until the chocolate has melted and become smooth. Beat in the butter and stir in the rum. Leave to cool and then place in the fridge for 3–4 hours or overnight.

2. For the macaroons, line two baking trays with baking parchment and fill a sink full of cold water. Tip the ground almonds and icing sugar into a food processor and blitz until they are very finely ground.

3. Sift the ground almond and sugar mix into a large bowl, using your fingers to rub the almonds through the mesh. Add half of the egg whites and mix well with a spatula or the tip of your fingers until smooth. Set aside.

4. Tip the 125g of caster sugar into a small saucepan and add 2 tablespoons of water. Heat gently until the sugar has dissolved and then slowly bring to the boil.

5. Meanwhile, pour the remaining egg whites into a large bowl with the salt and whisk with an electric hand mixer, gradually adding the 2 teaspoons of sugar, until it forms soft peaks.

6. Continue to heat the syrup until the sugar thermometer reads 117–120°C (this is known as the soft-ball stage; see page 14 for checking that this has been reached, especially if you don't have a sugar thermometer), lift the pan off the heat. Dip the bottom of the pan in the sink of cold water for a couple of seconds to stop it from continuing to cook. Alternatively, you could leave the pan for 25–30 seconds on a wire rack.

recipe continues ...

7. Pour the warm syrup gradually over the beaten egg white, slowly whisking with the hand mixer all the time. Continue to whisk until the meringue is nearly cold. Scrape half of the meringue onto the ground almond mixture and mix well using a rubber spatula (or a clean hand also works), then mix in the remaining meringue.

8. Now to 'macaronner', which is the classic French term for the scooping and folding motion that adds shine and elasticity to the macaroon mixture. To do this you'll need to use the spatula (or your hand) and keep turning the bowl and firmly folding the mixture for a lengthy 8–10 minutes.

9. Scrape some of the mixture into the piping bag fitted with the nozzle (be careful not to overfill as it will be tricky to pipe out) and pipe out the macaroons into 3–5cm rounds on the lined trays, leaving enough space between them to expand. Top up the bag as necessary. Set the trays aside for 30 minutes as this helps to create a crust on the outside.

10. Preheat the oven to 140°C/Gas mark 2 and bake the macaroons for 12–15 minutes. Remove from the oven and leave to cool on a wire rack.

11. Spoon a little of the ganache onto a macaroon and twist another macaroon onto the filling. Repeat with all the macaroons and put in the fridge overnight.

12. To decorate the macaroons, melt the white chocolate, brush it over the macaroons and sprinkle with the desiccated coconut.

GÜ TIP The reason why you put a macaroon in the fridge overnight is so it becomes chewy. You don't have to wait until morning to decorate it, though.

CHOCOLATE MACAROONS

What little gems these are. Pop one of these in your mouth and you'll soon be back for more. Make the macaroons the day before you are going to eat them and store in the fridge. This gives them their distinctive chewy texture.

MAKES ABOUT 25

100g dark chocolate (about 70% cocoa solids), broken into small pieces

125ml whipping cream

125g ground almonds

25g cocoa powder

150g icing sugar

3 large egg whites, lightly beaten

175g caster sugar

EQUIPMENT

Electric hand mixer

Sugar thermometer (optional)

Piping bag fitted with a 1cm piping nozzle

1. Make the filling first. Put the chocolate pieces into a heatproof bowl. Pour the cream into a saucepan and bring it to the boil. Pour it over the chocolate and stir with a spatula until the chocolate has melted and become smooth. Leave it stand for a few minutes, then cover the surface with cling film and set aside to cool.

2. For the macaroons, line two baking trays with baking parchment and fill a sink full of cold water. Tip the ground almonds, cocoa powder and icing sugar into a food processor and blitz until they are very finely ground.

3. Sift the ground almond and sugar mix into a large bowl, using your fingers to rub the almonds through the mesh. Add half of the egg whites and mix well with a spatula or the tip of your fingers until smooth. Set aside.

4. Whisk the remaining egg whites with an electric hand mixer in a bowl to soft peaks, then gradually whisk in 25g of the sugar until the mixture resembles shaving foam.

5. Tip the remaining 150g of the caster sugar into a small saucepan and add 3 tablespoons of water. Heat until the sugar has dissolved and then simmer gently.

6. When the syrup in the pan reaches 117–120°C on a sugar thermometer (this is known as the soft-ball stage; see page 14 for checking that this has been reached, especially if you don't have a sugar thermometer), lift the pan off the heat. Dip the bottom of the pan in the sink of cold water for a couple of seconds to stop it from continuing to cook. Alternatively, you could leave the pan for 25–30 seconds on a wire rack.

recipe continues ...

7. Pour the warm syrup gradually over the beaten egg white, slowly whisking with the hand mixer all the time. Continue to whisk until the meringue is nearly cold. Scrape half of the meringue onto the ground almond mixture and mix well using a rubber spatula (or a clean hand also works well), then mix in the remaining meringue.

8. Now to 'macaronner', which is the classic French term for the scooping and folding motion that adds shine and elasticity to the macaroon mixture. To do this you'll need to use the spatula (or your hand) and keep turning the bowl and firmly folding the mixture for a lengthy 8–10 minutes.

9. Scrape some of the mixture into the piping bag fitted with the nozzle (be careful not to overfill as it will be tricky to pipe out) and pipe out the macaroons into 3–5cm rounds on the lined trays, leaving enough space between them to expand. Top up the bag as necessary. Set the trays aside for 30 minutes as this helps to create a crust on the outside.

10. Preheat the oven to 140°C/Gas mark 2 and bake the macaroons for 12–15 minutes. Remove from the oven and leave to cool on a wire rack.

11. Spoon a little of the ganache onto a macaroon and twist another macaroon onto the filling. Repeat with all the macaroons and put in the fridge overnight.

CHOCOLATE CRÈME BRÛLÉE

A crème brûlée is a smooth and creamy custard that lies beneath a crispy, burnt sugar top. It is also known as crema Catalana, burnt cream or Trinity cream, but to our mind there is nothing so evocative as its French name, so we're sticking to it.

MAKES 4

4 egg yolks

75g caster sugar

100g dark chocolate (about 70% cocoa solids), broken into small pieces

250ml whipping cream

75ml milk

EQUIPMENT

4 x 100ml ramekins or other ovenproof dishes

Blow torch (optional)

1. Preheat the oven to 95°C/Gas mark lowest possible setting. Lightly beat the egg yolks with 50g of the sugar.

2. Put the chocolate pieces into a heatproof bowl. Pour the cream and milk into a saucepan and bring it to the boil. Pour the creamy milk over the chocolate and stir with a spatula until the chocolate has melted and become smooth. Add the chocolate mixture to the egg and sugar and stir well to combine.

3. Pour into the ramekins or other ovenproof dishes and bake for 30–40 minutes or until starting to puff at edges, but still wobbly in the centre. Leave to cool and then place in the fridge for 4–5 hours to chill completely.

4. Just before serving, preheat the grill to high and sprinkle the tops of the puddings evenly with the remaining sugar. You only need a thin layer of sugar to get a thin crunchy layer, so don't be tempted to add more. Place under the grill and cook until the sugar has dissolved and turned a golden brown colour. Alternatively, use a blow torch to melt the tops. Let the caramel set (which only takes a few minutes) and serve.

GÜ TIP Add the finely grated zest of an orange to the mix. Or add some very finely chopped chilli to the milk, bring to the boil and then leave to infuse for 30 minutes before straining into the cream and heating again.

GÜ TIP As much as we love our Gü glass ramekins, they can't be used twice in the oven, so please don't use them for these crème brûlées.

TWELFTH NIGHT CAKE

It is the tradition at Gü that Fred makes this quintessential French cake for Twelfth Night every year for all the staff. At the beginning of January, the patisseries and supermarkets in France are filled with this special gateau. The Twelfth Night Cake (or the 'galette des rois') is served in French homes on 6 January (hence, 'twelfth night') and should be cut into as many slices as there are people present, plus one extra slice, which was traditionally offered to the first poor person who pops in.

SERVES 10–12

125g unsalted butter, softened

125g caster sugar

2 eggs, plus 1 egg for glazing

125g ground almonds

125g dark chocolate (about 50% cocoa solids), broken into pieces

500g ready-made puff pastry

EQUIPMENT

Food processor or electric hand mixer

Coin or figurine

1. Preheat the oven to 190°C/Gas mark 5. Line a large baking tray with baking parchment.

2. Cream together the butter and sugar in the bowl of a food processor or with an electric hand mixer for about 5 minutes until they are light and fluffy. Add the eggs and ground almonds, and mix again until they are well combined. Melt the chocolate and stir in.

3. Divide the puff pastry in two and roll out each piece thinly on a lightly floured work surface. Using a large bowl with a diameter of about 30cm as a guide, cut out two discs. Roll one disc out again so it is about 1cm larger than the other.

4. Spread the chocolate almond cream onto the smaller disc of pastry, stopping about 3cm from the edge and press a coin or figurine randomly into the mixture.

5. Brush a little cold water around the edge of the pastry, cover with the remaining larger pastry disc and press the edges to seal.

6. Beat the egg for the glaze in a small bowl and brush it all over the top of the pastry. Using the back of a small knife, score the top of the pastry to create a simple pattern (being careful not to press too hard and pierce it). A traditional pattern would be to draw arcs from the centre of the cake to the edge, but do what ever takes your fancy.

7. Bake for 35–45 minutes or until it is well risen and golden brown. Traditionally, this cake is served with Champagne. Cheers to tradition!

GÜ TIP A simple variation would be to finely grate orange zest into the chocolate almond mix. You could also experiment with grinding other nuts to a powder in a food processor to replace the almonds. Pistachios are wonderful, and especially good served alongside some fresh cherries. To change the filling, replace the chocolate mix with a dry apple and vanilla purée to make a huge apple puff.

MELTING CHOCOLATE BOMBE

A dinner party surprise for you chocolate extremists. Presented as nothing more than chocolate domes on a plate, a warm chocolate sauce soon melts them to reveal homemade chocolate ice cream (although you could, of course, buy some in) adorned with caramel shards. The polycarbonate or silicone moulds that we suggest you use are available from good bakeware stores and websites (see page 17 for more information).

SERVES 6

FOR THE CHOCOLATE ICE CREAM

200g dark chocolate (about 70% cocoa solids), broken into small pieces

3 egg yolks

125g caster sugar

100ml whipped cream

500ml whole milk

2 tbsp liquid glucose or runny honey

FOR THE CHOCOLATE DOMES

250g dark chocolate (about 70% cocoa solids), broken into small pieces

1. To make the ice cream, put the chocolate pieces into a heatproof bowl and beat the egg yolks and sugar together in another heatproof bowl.

2. Put the cream, milk and glucose or honey into a saucepan and bring them to just below the boil. Pour two thirds of the hot mixture over the egg and sugar, whisking all the time.

3. Pour the mixture back into the pan and place over a low heat. Cook gently, stirring all the time, until the mixture thickens slightly. (Don't let it get too hot or it will curdle.)

4. Pour the hot custard through a sieve over the chocolate and whisk until it has melted and become smooth. Cover and chill in the fridge for a minimum of 4 hours for the flavour to mature.

5. Pour the custard into an ice-cream maker and churn to freeze. Alternatively, pour it into a plastic container and put it in the freezer, whisking well by hand every 30 minutes or so, until evenly slushy, then blitz it in a food processor. Return to the freezer for a further 30 minutes then blitz once more until smooth. Now freeze until set.

6. Now for the chocolate domes. Melt the chocolate as described on page 10 or, for a high shine on the chocolate, temper it using the technique described on page 193.

7. Brush a little melted chocolate evenly into your moulds, leave to set in the fridge, then repeat once more. Alternatively, blow up six balloons to about the size of a tennis ball and dip them into the melted chocolate. Shake off any excess and sit each balloon upside down in a cup. Then place in the fridge to set. Repeat once more.

FOR THE CARAMEL SHARDS

50g caster sugar

FOR THE CHOCOLATE SAUCE

100g dark chocolate (about 50% cocoa solids), broken into small pieces

200ml whipping cream

EQUIPMENT

Ice-cream maker or food processor

6 polycarbonate or silcone moulds the size of tennis balls or 6 small balloons

8. For the caramel shards, line a baking tray with baking parchment. Tip the sugar into a saucepan with 1 teaspoon of water. Heat gently for 3–4 minutes without stirring until the sugar has dissolved and turned a golden brown colour. Pour the caramel over the baking parchment, tipping the tray to get it as thin as possible.

9. For the sauce, put the chocolate pieces into a heatproof bowl. Pour the cream into a saucepan and bring it to the boil. Pour it over the chocolate and stir with a spatula until the chocolate has melted and become smooth.

10. To assemble, carefully unmould the chocolate domes out of the moulds or off the balloons. Scoop a generous ball of ice cream into the middle of the plate, stick a few shards of caramel into it. Pop a chocolate dome on top and serve immediately, pouring the hot chocolate sauce on top of domes at the table. Just watch those domes melt.

GÜ TIP The cocoa butter content in the chocolate will make the ice cream go very firm in the freezer after a few days, so it is always better to consume a homemade ice cream as soon as you can. It's a tough old world.

GÜ TIP You can flavour the ice cream with cinnamon, cardamom or chilli by infusing them in the milk for a few minutes. To take it up yet another level, put diced poached pear (see page 56) inside the dome with the ice cream or add ice cream-filled profiteroles (see page 22). For something a little simpler, crumble some broken cookies or chopped Caramelised Nuts (see page 37) over the ice cream in place of the caramel.

CHOCOLATE STUFFED CRUST PIZZA

Yes really! This is most definitely a pizza with a twist. It uses the recipe for Gü Classic Ganache, which is piped onto the dough edge and sealed in before baking. Once baked, it melts inside the crust, and squidges out when you bite into it. Heavenly! If your love of chocolate doesn't take you quite this far, however, then the stuffed crust is optional. As with a regular pizza, add toppings to your own taste – we've given you loads of ideas in the Gü tips on page 211.

MAKES 1 X 29CM ROUND PIZZA

100g homemade or shop-bought Gü Chocolate Ganache (see page 30) (optional)

2 tsp active dried yeast

250g plain flour

2 tbsp cocoa powder

1 tsp salt

3 tbsp olive oil, plus a trickle more

1 tbsp unsalted butter, melted

6 tbsp double cream

50g dark, milk or white chocolate, or a mixture of all three, finely chopped

2 tbsp toasted hazelnuts, roughly chopped

1 tbsp dark brown sugar

EQUIPMENT

Food processor

Piping bag fitted with a 1cm piping nozzle

1. Make (or buy) the Gü Chocolate Ganache, if using.

2. Pour 150ml of warm water into a small bowl, sprinkle with the yeast and leave to stand for about 5 minutes or until the yeast dissolves and starts to bubble.

3. Tip the flour, cocoa powder and salt into a food processor. Trickle in the oil and, with the machine running, pour in the yeast mixture and blend just until a dough forms. Turn the dough out onto a lightly floured surface (don't add too much flour here), and knead for only about a minute or until smooth.

4. Drop the dough into a large bowl, add a trickle of oil and turn the dough to coat. Cover and set aside in a warm, draft-free area for about an hour until the dough doubles in size.

5. Preheat the oven to 220°C/Gas mark 7 and place a baking sheet in to heat up to help to give your pizza a crispier base. Punch down the dough to remove any excess air (the perfect time to get rid of any excess frustration), and make it into a neat ball.

6. Roll out the dough on a lightly floured work surface to a 33cm circle. Fill your piping bag (or plastic bag) with the ganache, if using, and pipe a thin sausage all around the dough base, leaving a 2cm gap at the outside edge.

7. Brush a little water onto the dough around the inside of the ganache to dampen it, and roll over the outside of the dough, but not too tightly, to enclose the ganache. Press the inside edge to seal tightly.

8. Remove the hot baking tray from the oven and slide the dough base onto it. Brush all over with the melted butter and prick the centre lightly with a fork. Then bake for 10–15 minutes or until the edges are starting to brown and the centre is crispy.

9. Drizzle the centre with the cream, scatter with the chopped chocolate and nuts and sprinkle with the sugar. Put back in oven for a minute, just to warm and melt the topping.

recipe continues ...

GÜ TIP Use the raw dough straight away or at the end of Step 3 wrap it in cling film and keep it in the fridge until the next day. Just punch it down again and use as above.

GÜ TOPPINGS Go on, embrace variety: add a sprinkling of cocoa powder or a little Citrus Dust (see page 38); a slather of Chocolate Praline Spread (see page 52) or crumbled pieces of Sesame Nougatine (see page 32). The choice is yours!

CHOCOLATE & BACON CROQUE MONSIEUR

Trust us – chocolate and bacon are a perfect match. Here is a traditional French brasserie classic with a Gü chocolate twist – the savoury chocolate jam is delicious.

SERVES 4

8 streaky bacon rashers

8 slices of white bread with the crust removed

200g Comte or Emmental cheese, grated

FOR THE CHOCOLATE JAM

2 tbsp vegetable oil

5 shallots, peeled and finely chopped

2 tbsp balsamic vinegar

2 tbsp caster sugar

200ml red wine

Salt and freshly ground black pepper

25g dark chocolate (about 70% cocoa solids), finely chopped

FOR THE WHITE SAUCE

500ml milk

50g unsalted butter

50g plain flour

Grated nutmeg

1. To make the chocolate jam, heat the oil in a small saucepan over a low heat. Add the chopped shallots and cook for about 10 minutes, stirring occasionally, until they are very soft and translucent.

2. Pour in the balsamic vinegar, then add the sugar and red wine and season with salt and pepper. Bring to the boil and then let it reduce until the liquid has nearly evaporated. Stir the chopped chocolate into the hot jam and mix well. Remove from the heat and leave to cool.

3. For the white sauce, heat the milk to just under boiling in a saucepan and then remove it from the heat. Melt the butter in a separate saucepan over a low heat. Add the flour and stir the mixture with a spatula for about 2 minutes or until it looks sandy. Slowly pour the hot milk into the butter/flour mixture and cook for 1–2 minutes, stirring constantly, until the sauce has thickened. Remove from the heat and season with salt, pepper and nutmeg.

4. To finish, grill the bacon and toast the bread. Leave the grill switched on at full. Spread a slice of toast with some of the white sauce and top with two bacon slices. Spread the other slice with a little chocolate jam and turn and press gently on top of the bacon.

5. Spoon more white sauce over the croque monsieur, sprinkle over some cheese and place under the grill. The finished article is great served with dressed salad leaves sprinkled with toasted nuts.

WHOLE CHICKEN IN A COCOA CRUST

WITH VANILLA MASH AND DARK CHOCOLATE GRAVY

A recipe with a wow factor to impress your friends. Not only will your guests be blown away by the sight of this dish, but the cocoa crust creates delicious, moist and very tender chicken underneath.

SERVES 4–6

2–2.5kg whole chicken, wings and ends of legs removed for the gravy

1 lemon

FOR THE COCOA CRUST

500g plain flour

100g cocoa powder

250g salt

3 egg whites

FOR THE CHOCOLATE GRAVY

1 tbsp vegetable oil

½ onion, peeled and chopped

½ carrot, peeled and chopped

1 small chilli, deseeded and chopped

1 tsp plain flour

2 tbsp white wine

450ml hot chicken stock

20g dark chocolate (about 50% cocoa solids), chopped into small pieces

½ tsp lemon juice

½ tbsp unsalted butter

FOR THE MASH

100ml whipping cream

25g unsalted butter

Salt and white pepper

2 vanilla pods or 4 tsp vanilla extract

700g floury potatoes, such as Maris Piper or King Edward

1. To make the cocoa crust, sift the flour and cocoa powder into a large bowl and stir in the salt. Lightly beat the egg whites with 250ml of cold water and then stir them into the dry mixture with a fork. Bring together to form a firm dough and knead for about a minute until smooth. Cover the dough with cling film and leave to rest for 10 minutes.

2. Lift the skin of the chicken breast and wiggle your fingers underneath to loosen. Season with a little salt and pepper and place the whole lemon in its cavity.

3. Preheat the oven to 180°C/Gas mark 4. Using one third of the cocoa dough, roll it out on baking parchment so it's about 5cm bigger than the chicken all round. Place in a roasting tin and position the chicken in the middle. Brush the edges with a little water.

4. Roll the remaining dough to about 5mm thick and large enough to cover the chicken. Place it on top of the chicken and seal the dough by pressing gently all around it.

5. Bake the chicken for 18 minutes per 500g, plus 30 minutes or until the juices that run from the chicken and seeping out of the dough are clear.

6. In the last 45 minutes make the gravy and the mash. For the gravy, heat the oil in a saucepan over a medium heat and brown the chicken trimmings all over. Scoop the trimmings out and set aside. Add the onion, carrot and chilli to the pan and cook for 5–6 minutes, stirring occasionally, until golden. If there is any excess fat in the bottom of the pan, scoop out with a tablespoon.

recipe continues ...

7. Return the trimmings to the pan, sprinkle with the flour, mix well and cook for about a minute. Add the white wine, let it bubble up and simmer until reduced by half. Then pour in the stock and reduce by half again. Pass the sauce through a sieve into a clean pan and set aside.

8. Meanwhile, for the mash, pour the cream into a small saucepan, add the butter and season well with salt and pepper. Split the vanilla pods in half lengthways, if using, scrape the seeds from their middle into the cream and drop in the pods. Bring to the boil, remove from heat, cover and leave to infuse.

9. Peel the potatoes and cut into chunks of equal size, then rinse with cold water and place in a saucepan. Cover with more cold water and add a pinch of salt. Cover with a lid and bring to the boil, then reduce the heat and simmer for 15–20 minutes or until the potatoes are tender.

10. Drain the potatoes and then mash thoroughly. Slowly add the vanilla cream through a sieve and beat well. Check and adjust the seasoning and keep warm.

11. Gently reheat the gravy and stir in the chocolate. Check the seasoning and add lemon juice to taste. Whisk in the butter and keep warm.

12. When the chicken is ready, place it on a serving dish and carry it over to the table. Cut open the crust and discard – very theatrical! Carve the chicken in front of your guests, such an impressive sight. Serve the vanilla mash and chocolate gravy on the side together with some steamed beans, peas or carrots.

ACKNOWLEDGEMENTS

There's a whole heap of thanks that need to go out to all the brilliant people who helped to turn the Gü Chocolate Cookbook from an exciting idea into this beautiful book just a few months later... Most importantly, thanks to our fantastic chefs, Fred and Jerome, who worked so hard on creating all these amazing (and sometimes slightly bonkers) recipes, ably assisted by Annie Nichols and Emma Callery. To all the HarperCollins team especially Lizzy, Helen and Myfanwy who put their hearts and souls into the project. To the wonderful stylists, Kim Morphew and Cynthia Inions, for creating such stunning and delicious spreads. To our incredibly talented photographer, Maya Smend, who shot all this beautiful, crave-worthy, chocolatey loveliness. To the Gü girls who have tag teamed on bringing the brand to life – especially Lizzie H-T, Sarah, Polly and Ellie. And to the extended family Fennell for being patient proofreaders and tasters extraordinaire whenever called upon in the service of chocolate.

INDEX

A

almonds: chocolate financiers 66
  chocolate macaroons 201–2
  chocolate praline spread 52
  piña colada macaroons 198–200
  profiteroles with almond
    Chantilly cream 180
  Twelfth Night cake 205
apricots: sticky chocolatey toffee pud 140
avocados: banana and avocado cream 157

B

bacon: chocolate and bacon
  croque monsieur 211
baking beans 12
baking blind 12
baking parchment 15
baking sheets and trays 15
bananas: banana and avocado cream 157
  banana spring rolls 165
  caramelised banana split 103
beef: Gü-lash 152
beetroot: chocolate blinis with smoked
  salmon 182
birthday cake, chocolate sponge 176
biscuits: Viennese biscuits 96
  see also cookies; digestive biscuits
Black Forest fondants 128
blackberries: summer berry chutney 160
blinis, chocolate 182
blondies, white chocolate 68
blueberries: summer berry chutney 160
bombe, melting chocolate 206–7
boozy cherry chocolate clafoutis 127

bread: chocolate and bacon croque monsieur 211
  chocolate grissini 53
bread and butter pudding, pain au chocolat 133
brioche: caramelised brioche croûtons 116
  Easter eggs 162
brownies: brownie fingers 104
  chocolate, fig and pear trifle 137
  macadamia nut brownies 72
  raspberry chocolate mousse pots 110
bubble wrap, chocolate 194
butter 9

C

cake testers 16
cake tins, buttering and lining 12
cakes: brownie fingers 104
  chocolate financiers 66
  chocolate madeleines 99
  chocolate marzipan cake 71
  chocolate sponge birthday cake 176
  easy chocolate mousse cake 169–70
  Gü-ey dark chocolate fudge cake 86
  Güpcakes with chocolate ganache frosting
    65–6
  macadamia nut brownies 72
  white chocolate blondies 68
candied citrus fruit 36
  Jaffa cake lollipops 74
caramel 13
  caramel shards 206–7
  caramelised banana split 103
  caramelised brioche croûtons 116
  caramelised nuts 37
  caramelised popcorn or puffed rice 34

chocolate and pear tarte tatin 130
chocolate caramels 100
chocolate crème brûlée 203
chocolate tiffin 81
floating islands 50–2
millionaire's flapjack 112
salted caramel and peanut tart 166
salted caramel custard 27
salted caramel sauce 26
sesame nougatine 32
sticky chocolatey toffee pud 140
white chocolate and coffee crème brûlée 118
white chocolate parfait 142
cardamom pods: chocolate, cardamom and
  clementine marbled roulade 172
  milk chocolate, orange and cardamom
    truffles 94
Chantilly cream 20
  chocolate Chantilly cream 197
  coconut snowball profiteroles 190
  hot chocolate with orange Chantilly cream 48
  profiteroles with almond Chantilly cream 180
  white chocolate Eton mess 148
cheese: chocolate and bacon croque
  monsieur 211
  see also mascarpone cheese
cheesecakes: chocolate cheesecake 82
  white chocolate cheesecake 160
cherries: Black Forest fondants 128
  boozy cherry chocolate clafoutis 127
chewy double chocolate cookies 60
chicken: whole chicken in a cocoa crust
  212–14
chilli, hot chocolate with 49
choux pastry 22–3

chocolate éclairs 62
  coconut snowball profiteroles 190
  craquelin topping 22–3
  profiteroles with almond Chantilly cream 180
churros 44
chutney, summer berry 160
citrus dust 38
citrus fruit, candied 36
clafoutis, boozy cherry chocolate 127
clementines: chocolate, cardamom and
  clementine marbled roulade 172
cocoa solids 8
coconut: coconut snowball profiteroles 190
  piña colada macaroons 198–200
  white chocolate and coconut meringues 167–8
  white chocolate and wasabi truffles 95
coffee: coffee ice cream 90
  tiramigü 144
  white chocolate and coffee crème brûlée 118
confectionery: chocolate caramels 100
  chocolate truffles 92
  milk chocolate, orange and cardamom
    truffles 94
  white chocolate and wasabi truffles 95
cookies: chewy double chocolate cookies 60
  chocolate, ginger and sesame cookies 76
  chocolate, peanut and nougat cookies 78
  triple chocolate cookies 109
  see also biscuits
craquelin topping, choux pastry with 22–3
cream 10
  Chantilly cream 20
  chocolate and peach knickerbocker glory 178
  chocolate Chantilly cream 197

chocolate fondue 165–6
chocolate mousse 141
creamy chocolate custard 24, 62
Gü chocolate milkshake 108
hot chocolate with chilli 49
hot chocolate with orange Chantilly cream 48
pot au chocolat 123
thick hot chocolate 48
warm rum chocolate ganache 103
white chocolate parfait 142
crème brûlée: chocolate crème brûlée 203
  white chocolate and coffee crème brûlée 118
crème de cacao: chocolate martini 147
croque monsieur, chocolate and bacon 211
croûtons, caramelised brioche 116
crumble, chocolate pecan 31
curls, chocolate 12
custard 13
  chocolate crème brûlée 203
  creamy chocolate custard 24, 62
  floating islands 50–2
  salted caramel custard 27
  white chocolate and coffee crème brûlée 118

D
dark chocolate 8
dates: sticky chocolatey toffee pud 140
digestive biscuits: chocolate cheesecake 82
  chocolate tiffin 81
  rocky road 85
  white chocolate cheesecake 160
domes, chocolate 206–7
double cream 10
doughnuts: churros 44

dressing, chocolate 186
drinks: chocolate martini 147
  Gü chocolate milkshake 108
  hot chocolate with chilli 49
  hot chocolate with orange Chantilly cream 48
  thick hot chocolate 48
duck: pan-fried duck on polenta 185

E
Easter eggs 162
easy chocolate mousse cake 169–70
éclairs 22–3
  chocolate éclairs 62
eggs 9
  custard 13
  whisking whites 14
electrical equipment 14–15
equipment 14–17
Eton mess, white chocolate 148

F
fennel sauce 181
figs: chocolate, fig and pear trifle 137
financiers, chocolate 66
flapjack, millionaire's 112
floating islands 50–2
fondant, chocolate 128
fondue, chocolate 165–6
food processors 15
fritters: churros 44
frosting, chocolate ganache 65–6
fudge cake, Gü-ey dark chocolate 86

G

ganache: chocolate ganache 30
  Güpcakes with chocolate ganache frosting
    65–6
  piña colada macaroons 198–200
  raspberry ganache tart 120
  warm rum chocolate ganache 103
gelatine 10
ginger: chocolate, ginger and sesame cookies 76
  mini pear, ginger and chocolate tarts 56
glaze, rich chocolate 169–70
Grand Marnier: citrus dust 38
grapefruit: candied citrus fruit 36
graters 16
gravy, chocolate 212–14
grissini, chocolate 53
Gü chocolate milkshake 108
Gü-ey dark chocolate fudge cake 86
Gü-lash 152
Güpcakes with chocolate ganache frosting
  65–6

H

hazelnuts: brownie fingers 104
  chocolate financiers 66
  chocolate praline spread 52
herb salad 155–6
hot chocolate, thick 48
hot chocolate with chilli 49
hot chocolate with orange Chantilly cream 48

I

ice cream: chocolate and peach
  knickerbocker glory 178
  chocolate ice cream lollipops 107–8
  coffee ice cream 90
  Gü chocolate milkshake 108
  melting chocolate bombe 206–7
ice-cream machines 15
icing: chocolate ganache frosting 65–6
  chocolate glaze 176
  rich chocolate glaze 169–70
iles flottante 50–2
ingredients 9–10
irresistible chocolate tart 124

J

Jaffa cake lollipops 74
jam, chocolate 211

K

Kirsch: Black Forest fondants 128
  boozy cherry chocolate clafoutis 127
knickerbocker glory, chocolate and peach 178

L

lemons, poached 182
lining cake tins 12
lollipops: chocolate ice cream lollipops 107–8
  Jaffa cake lollipops 74
  spiral chocolate lollipops 175

M

macadamia nut brownies 72
macaroons: chocolate macaroons 201–2
  piña colada macaroons 198–200
madeleines, chocolate 99
mangoes: chocolate, marmalade, mango
    and pine nut tart 79
  coconut snowball profiteroles 190

Easter eggs 162
marmalade: chocolate, marmalade,
    mango and pine nut tart 79
  Jaffa cake lollipops 74
Marsala: chocolate, fig and pear trifle 137
marshmallows: rocky road 85
martini, chocolate 147
marzipan: chocolate marzipan cake 71
  profiteroles with almond Chantilly cream 180
mascarpone cheese: chocolate, fig and pear
    trifle 137
  tiramigü 144
measuring spoons 9
melt in the middle 138
melting chocolate 10
melting chocolate bombe 206–7
meringues 14
  chocolate, cardamom and clementine
    marbled roulade 172
  dark chocolate meringues 167–8
  floating islands 50–2
  white chocolate and coconut meringues
    167–8
  white chocolate Eton mess 148
Microplane graters 16
microwave ovens: melting chocolate 10
  tempering chocolate 193
milk 9
  chocolate rice pudding 105
  Gü chocolate milkshake 108
milk chocolate 8
  caramelised banana split 103
  chocolate Chantilly cream 197
  chocolate chip pancakes 55

chocolate fondue 165
chocolate ganache icing 65
chocolate praline spread 52
chocolate stuffed crust pizza 208–11
Gü chocolate ganache 30
hot chocolate with chilli 49
milk chocolate, orange and cardamom
    truffles 94
rocky road 85
spiral chocolate lollipops 175
thick hot chocolate 48
triple chocolate cookies 109
millefeuille, chocolate 197
millionaire's flapjack 112
mint sugar 148
mixers, electric 14–15
monkfish with a chocolate and shallot
    salad and fennel sauce 181
mousses: chocolate mousse 141
  easy chocolate mousse cake 169–70
  raspberry chocolate mousse pots 110
  warm chocolate mousse 90–2
muffins, chocolate and pecan 43
mushrooms: rabbit ragü 151

N
nougat: chocolate, peanut and nougat
  cookies 78
nougatine, sesame 32
nozzles, piping 16
nuts: caramelised nuts 37
  see also almonds, hazelnuts etc

O

oats: millionaire's flapjack 112

open dark chocolate venison raviole 155–6

oranges: candied citrus fruit 36

chocolate, cardamom and clementine marbled roulade 172

chocolate orange sauce 185

citrus dust 38

hot chocolate with orange Chantilly cream 48

milk chocolate, orange and cardamom truffles 94

oven temperatures 9

P

pain au chocolat bread and butter pudding 133

pancakes, chocolate chip 55

parfait, white chocolate 142

parsnips: white chocolate and parsnip purée 151

passion fruit: Easter eggs 162

pasta: open dark chocolate venison raviole 155–6

pastries: banana spring rolls 165

chocolate éclairs 62

chocolate millefeuille 197

coconut snowball profiteroles 190

profiteroles with almond Chantilly cream 180

Twelfth Night cake 205

pastry: baking blind 12

chocolate sweetcrust pastry 29–30

choux pastry 22–3

peaches: chocolate and peach knickerbocker glory 178

peanut butter: salted caramel and peanut tart 166

peanuts: chocolate, peanut and nougat cookies 78

white chocolate parfait 142

pears: chocolate and pear tarte tatin 130

chocolate, fig and pear trifle 137

mini pear, ginger and chocolate tarts 56

pecan nuts: chocolate and pecan muffins 43

chocolate pecan crumble 31

peppers: Gü-lash 152

pestle and mortar 16

piña colada macaroons 198–200

pine nuts: chocolate, marmalade, mango and pine nut tart 79

pineapple: piña colada macaroons 198–200

roast pineapple 165

piping bags 16

pizza, chocolate stuffed crust 208–11

polenta, pan-fried duck on 185

polycarbonate moulds 17

popcorn, caramelised 34

pork mole 157

pot au chocolat 123

potatoes: vanilla mash 212–14

praline spread, chocolate 52

profiteroles 22–3

coconut snowball profiteroles 190

profiteroles with almond Chantilly cream 180

puffed rice: caramelised puffed rice 34

rocky road 85

R

rabbit ragü 151

ramekins 16

raspberries: chocolate and peach knickerbocker glory 178

raspberry chocolate mousse pots 110

raspberry ganache tart 120

summer berry chutney 160

raviole, open dark chocolate venison 155–6

rice pudding, chocolate 105

rocky road 85

roulade, chocolate, cardamom and

clementine marbled 172

rubber spatulas 16

rum chocolate ganache 103

S

sabayon sauce 13

salad, chocolate and shallot 181

salted caramel and peanut tart 166

salted caramel custard 27

salted caramel sauce 26

sauces: chocolate ganache 30

chocolate gravy 212–14

chocolate orange sauce 185

chocolate sauce 178, 206–7

creamy chocolate custard 24, 62

custard 13

sabayon sauce 13

salted caramel custard 27

salted caramel sauce 26

sticky chocolatey toffee sauce 140

white sauce 211

scales 17

scallops with a sesame crust and

chocolate dressing 186

sesame seeds: chocolate, ginger and

sesame cookies 76

scallops with a sesame crust and

chocolate dressing 186

sesame nougatine 32

shallots: chocolate and shallot salad 181

silicone mats 15

silicone moulds 17

smoked salmon, chocolate blinis with 182

soufflé, chocolate 134

soup, chocolate 116

spatulas 16

spiral chocolate lollipops 175

sponge: chocolate sponge 169–70

chocolate sponge birthday cake 176

chocolate sponge fingers 144

spread, chocolate praline 52

spring rolls, banana 165

stews: Gü-lash 152

open dark chocolate venison raviole 155–6

rabbit ragü 151

stick blenders 15

sticky chocolatey toffee pud 140

strawberries: white chocolate Eton mess 148

sugar: caramel 13

mint sugar 148

sugar syrup 14

sugar thermometers 14, 17

sultanas: chocolate tiffin 81

rocky road 85

summer berry chutney 160

sweetcrust pastry, chocolate 29–30

syrup, sugar 14

T

tarts: chocolate and pear tarte tatin 130

chocolate, marmalade, mango and

pine nut tart 79

irresistible chocolate tart 124

mini pear, ginger and chocolate tarts 56
raspberry ganache tart 120
salted caramel and peanut tart 166
temperatures, oven 9
tempering chocolate 193
thermometers, sugar 14, 17
tiffin, chocolate 81
tiramigü 144
toffee: sticky chocolatey toffee pud 140
tomatoes: pork mole 157
trifle, chocolate, fig and pear 137
triple chocolate cookies 109
truffles: chocolate truffles 92
  milk chocolate, orange and cardamom
    truffles 94
  white chocolate and wasabi truffles 95
Twelfth Night cake 205

V
vanilla mash 212–14
venison: open dark chocolate venison
  raviole 155–6
Viennese biscuits 96
vodka: chocolate martini 147

W
waffles, chocolate 46
wasabi: white chocolate and wasabi truffles 95
weighing scales 17
whipping cream 10
whisking egg whites 14
white chocolate 8
  chocolate and peach knickerbocker glory 178
  chocolate chip pancakes 55

chocolate stuffed crust pizza 208–11
Easter eggs 162
piña colada macaroons 198–200
spiral chocolate lollipops 175
triple chocolate cookies 109
white chocolate and coconut meringues
  167–8
white chocolate and coffee crème brûlée 118
white chocolate and parsnip purée 151
white chocolate and wasabi truffles 95
white chocolate blondies 68
white chocolate cheesecake 160
white chocolate Eton mess 148
white chocolate parfait 142
white sauce 211
wine: chocolate, fig and pear trifle 137
  Gü-lash 152
  open dark chocolate venison raviole 155–6

ABOUT THE GÜ CHEFS

Hello – I'm Fred. My journey to becoming Gü's head chef started from a very early age when I used to help my grandmother make chocolate mousse; her actual mousse recipe is in this book. However, my biggest food influence was my uncle Hubert, who grew all sorts of vegetables and fruit. When I was 7, I received what I still consider to be the best gift any kid could get for Christmas: a full box of my uncle's fruit and veg, each of them individually wrapped.

I started my training as a pastry chef at the age of 14 after a chocolatier visited my school to talk about his skills. My first day in the pastry shop ended up with my boss accidentally splashing a large amount of chocolate on my brand new chef's whites – it was a chocolate blessing and since then it's always been about chocolate. My life-long love of desserts and chocolate took me to Paris, Northern France and finally Gü in 2003. My son Matt is also a big, big chocolate lover – I hope this book shares with him (and with home cooks everywhere) my passion for all things chocolate and provides inspiration to experiment with this fantastic ingredient.

Hi – I'm Jerome. I grew up in Southwest France surrounded by great food. As a child, I learned from my parents to love and cook great local dishes like cassoulet, confit duck and ceps mushrooms and we would all pick fruit and veg from the garden to go in these dishes. Every Sunday my mum would cook the roast chicken and in the early summer my favourite Sunday lunch dessert was chocolate and cherry clafoutis – just like the one in this book.

I started my career as a trainee chef for four years in France then changed to the sweet side after working for Michel Belin award-winning chocolatier in Albi. Later on I moved to Paris and worked for three Michelin-starred chefs – Bernard Pacaud, Philippe Legendre and the legendary Pierre Gagnaire. In 2010 I finally joined Gü to be the second in command to Fred.